The Challenge for Research in Higher Education:
Harmonizing Excellence and Utility

by Alan W. Lindsay and Ruth T. Neumann

ASHE-ERIC Higher Education Report No. 8, 1988

Prepared by

Clearinghouse on Higher Education
The George Washington University

Published by

Association for the Study of
Higher Education

Jonathan D. Fife,
Series Editor

Cite as
Lindsay, Alan W., and Ruth T. Neumann. *The Challenge for Research in Higher Education: Harmonizing Excellence and Utility.* ASHE-ERIC Higher Education Report No. 8. Washington, D.C.: Association for the Study of Higher Education, 1988.

Library of Congress Catalog Card Number 89-83630
ISSN 0884-0040
ISBN 0-913317-52–7

Managing Editor: Christopher Rigaux
Manuscript Editor: Barbara Fishel/Editech
Cover design by Michael David Brown, Rockville, Maryland

The ERIC Clearinghouse on Higher Education invites individuals to submit proposals for writing monographs for the Higher Education Report series. Proposals must include:
1. A detailed manuscript proposal of not more than five pages.
2. A chapter-by-chapter outline.
3. A 75-word summary to be used by several review committees for the initial screening and rating of each proposal.
4. A vita.
5. A writing sample.

[ERIC] **Clearinghouse on Higher Education**
School of Education and Human Development
The George Washington University
One Dupont Circle, Suite 630
Washington, D.C. 20036-1183

ASHE **Association for the Study of Higher Education**
Texas A&M University
Department of Educational Administration
Harrington Education Center
College Station, Texas 77843

This publication was prepared partially with funding from the Office of Educational Research and Improvement, U.S. Department of Education, under contract no. ED RI-88-062014. The opinions expressed in this report do not necessarily reflect the positions or policies of OERI or the Department.

EXECUTIVE SUMMARY

Over the last decade, university research has gradually changed its character under the influence of cost pressures, ambivalent public attitudes, and increasingly narrow notions of "utility." The natural sciences have received higher priority, and research has been increasingly concentrated in large teams and centers. The proportion of applied research has increased and closer links with industry developed. These trends have contributed to a weakening of the teaching-research nexus. Relationships with government have been marked by increasing bureaucratization and control. The business community and the government both stress the contribution of university research to national economic and social renewal, but the pattern of postwar development in higher education has brought utility into conflict with excellence, the traditional criterion for funding research. The challenge is to incorporate utility into research policy and funding without compromising the pursuit of excellence.

This study examines the changing notions of excellence and utility and their influence on the purposes and culture of higher education. The many faces of excellence and utility are explored within the pattern of higher education's development. Higher education has prospered when excellence and utility have been in harmony and faltered when they have come into conflict. The major focus of the study is on the narrowing of meaning that has occurred since World War II and how excellence and utility now tend to operate in conflict within the research policy and funding processes. From an understanding of this conflict and the damage it is causing, proposals for reharmonizing excellence and utility are developed.

What Do the Notions of "Excellence" and "Utility" Mean?

Excellence and utility are powerful words with many shades of meaning. Excellence denotes a superlative performance—one superior to other performers. From early times, the pursuit of excellence has been linked with moral and intellectual qualities. In higher education, it has been generalized into a self-justifying goal rather separated from the consideration of "excellence in what?" Utility refers to the capacity to yield benefits or satisfy wants. It indicates suitability for some purpose rather than inherent attributes.

How Have Notions of Excellence and Utility in Higher Education Changed over Time?

Excellence and utility have always been central concepts in higher education, although their meaning and relative importance have changed over time. The classical Greek notion of excellence as the conjunction of virtue and knowledge was readily assimilated into the medieval university as intellectual virtuosity achieved through the rigorous use of logic. With the 19th century reforms under the impetus of the German model, excellence became identified with the advancement at the highest level of knowledge for its own sake. Since then, notions of excellence in higher education have tended to be self-justifying and have become rather divorced from human purposes. The expansion of basic research under government patronage after World War II reinforced this trend and led to an inward-looking, discipline-oriented, single-criterion view of excellence.

While excellence has been a central concern within the university, the periods of expansion and development in higher education have been directed by utilitarian considerations. The utility of universities has at various times resided in the mastery of established dogmas, the cultivation of minds and manners, the discovery of new knowledge, and the solving of practical problems in society. Since World War II, the increasing importance of university research to economic goals has led to a greater emphasis on utility. With the economic decline in more recent years, the notion of utility has become more restricted in focus and time to mean having immediate applications with economic benefits. Nevertheless, universities have historically flourished and served their societies best when they have been engaged in the pursuit of excellence.

How Is Higher Education's Role in Research Changing?
Research in higher education is characterized by diverse orientations and approaches. Significant differences across the disciplines provide the problems and framework for most research. Recently, the notion of research has narrowed, differentiating it from "scholarship" through an emphasis on the "new" knowledge of the sciences. Trends in policy and funding have favored a restricted view of research, the separation of research and teaching, and in particular those sciences with immediate economic or military utility. Belief in the benefits of a strong connection between university research and teaching has long been an article of faith in American higher education, especially at the graduate level. Certainly, teaching and research have historically developed in close relationship, but they now have both connections and conflicts between them.

Are Excellence and Utility in Harmony or Conflict?

During much of the development of higher education, excellence and utility have tended to be harmonious, but the narrowing of meaning in recent times has brought them more and more into conflict. At the macro level, governments and industry, in seeking to harness the resources of the universities in the quest for economic prosperity, value research with immediate applications, while at the micro level, researchers, at least in the more traditional disciplines, adhere to excellence in contributing to knowledge as a self-justifying criterion. This exclusive commitment to following the dictates of the discipline and the resulting neglect of problem solving is at the heart of the conflict between excellence and utility.

What Are the Implications for Policy and Management?

In summary, the fertile research system in American higher education is being weakened by:

1. a narrowing of the notions of excellence and utility,
2. a narrowing of the notion of "research" to differentiate it from "scholarship,"
3. an undermining of the university research culture, and
4. a loosening of connection between teaching and research.

All the major groups involved—faculty, institutional leaders and administrators, policy makers, and the sponsors and users of research—must act to counter these trends and to achieve a greater degree of harmony between excellence and utility.

The strategies necessary to meet the challenge are encapsulated in 14 recommendations:

1. Criteria of both excellence and utility should be incorporated into the assessment of research proposals. Criteria for excellence should encompass outstanding contributions to solving society's problems as well as to the advancement of knowledge; those for utility should encompass social and cultural contributions as well as economic, indirect and long term as well as short term and direct.
2. The terms "research" and "scholarship" should be regarded as describing essentially the same general process common to all disciplines.

3. The distinction between basic and applied should be recognized as an artificial one that hampers rather than assists an understanding of the relevance of research.
4. The range of approaches to research and disciplinary perspectives should be maintained without reductions of support for fields whose utility is less immediately apparent.
5. Although peer review is fundamental to the systematic advancement of knowledge, research review panels should not be restricted to the most immediate peer group of fellow researchers but should always include researchers from related fields and, in some cases, the general academic community.
6. Researchers with substantial commercial interests in a research topic should not be involved in the assessment of proposals.
7. Institutions should be more responsive in balancing the competing interests of their constituencies and ensuring that short-term commercial considerations do not dominate decisions to the exclusion of social and cultural concerns.
8. Institutional reward structures should be revised to reflect the many different contributions a faculty member can make.
9. New forms of organization must be encouraged to link the frontiers of knowledge to society's problems, but the strengths of traditional disciplinary departments should not be forgotten. Barriers against bureaucratization, aversion to taking risks, and the application of undue political and economic pressures need to be strengthened.
10. Greater collegial responsibility should be taken for the assessment of standards, social and economic implications, and ethical behavior.
11. National needs and priorities should be determined through wide consultation and debate among the interest groups involved.
12. The very successful university research culture should not be compromised in efforts to improve relationships with industry.
13. The teaching-research nexus should remain central to the function of universities. University teaching, at all lev-

els, must not become divorced from its source—open-minded inquiry.

14. A pool of researchers and the associated infrastructure should be maintained in each field, regardless of current and often transient priorities, in recognition of the time required to develop expertise and leadership in research.

ADVISORY BOARD

Roger G. Baldwin
Assistant Professor of Education
College of William and Mary

Carol M. Boyer
Consultant and Senior Academic Planner
Massachusetts Board of Regents of Higher Education

Ellen Earle Chaffee
Associate Commissioner for Academic Affairs
North Dakota Board of Higher Education

Elaine H. El-Khawas
Vice President
Policy Analysis and Research
American Council on Education

Martin Finkelstein
Associate Professor of Higher Education Administration
Seton Hall University

Carol Everly Floyd
Associate Vice Chancellor for Academic Affairs
Board of Regents of the Regency Universities System
State of Illinois

George D. Kuh
Professor of Higher Education
School of Education
Indiana University

Yvonna S. Lincoln
Associate Professor of Higher Education
University of Kansas

Richard F. Wilson
Associate Chancellor
University of Illinois

Ami Zusman
Principal Analyst, Academic Affairs
University of California

CONSULTING EDITORS

Charles Adams
Director, The Inquiry Program
Center for the Study of Adult and Higher Education
University of Massachusetts

Ann E. Austin
Research Assistant Professor
Vanderbilt University

Robert J. Barak
Deputy Executive Secretary
Director of Academic Affairs and Research
Iowa Board of Regents

Robert Berdahl
Professor of Higher Education
University of Maryland

Kenneth A. Bruffee
Director, The Scholars Program
Brooklyn College of the City University of New York

L. Leon Campbell
Provost and Vice President for Academic Affairs
University of Delaware

Robert Paul Churchill
Chair and Associate Professor
Department of Philosophy
George Washington University

Charles S. Claxton
Associate Professor
Center for the Study of Higher Education
Memphis State University

Susan Cohen
Associate, Project for Collaborative Learning
Lesley College

John W. Creswell
Professor and Lilly Project Director
University of Nebraska

Andre Deruyttere
Vice President
Catholic University at Leuven, Belgium

Irwin Feller
Director, Institute for Policy Research and Evaluation
Pennsylvania State University

Zelda F. Gamson
Director
New England Resource Center for Higher Education

Kenneth C. Green
Associate Director
Higher Education Research Institute
University of California at Los Angeles

Milton Greenberg
Provost
American University

Judith Dozier Hackman
Associate Dean
Yale University

Brian L. Hawkins
Vice President for Computing and Information Services
Brown University

Lynn G. Johnson
Executive Director
Hudson-Mohawk Association of Colleges and Universities

Carl J. Lange
Vice President for Research
George Washington University

Oscar T. Lenning
Vice President for Academic Affairs
Robert Wesleyan College

Judith B. McLaughlin
Research Associate on Education and Sociology
Harvard University

Andrew T. Masland
Judicial/Public Safety Market Manager
Digital Equipment Corporation

Marcia Mentkowski
Director of Research and Evaluation
Professor of Psychology
Alverno College

Richard I. Miller
Professor, Higher Education
Ohio University

James R. Mingle
Executive Director
State Higher Education Executive Officers

Elizabeth M. Nuss
Executive Director
National Association of Student Personnel Administrators

Anne M. Pratt
Director for Foundation Relations
College of William and Mary

Karen T. Romer
Associate Dean for Academic Affairs
Brown University

Jack E. Rossmann
Professor of Psychology
Macalester College

Donald M. Sacken
Associate Professor
University of Arizona

Robert A. Scott
President
Ramapo College of New Jersey

Mary Ann Sheridan
Director of Sponsored Programs
Ohio State University Research Foundation

J. Fredericks Volkwein
Director of Institutional Research
State University of New York at Albany

William R. Whipple
Director, Honors Program
University of Maine

CONTENTS

FOREWORD

The concepts discussed in this report are especially timely, as higher education prepares to enter a new decade and the federal government, under a new administration, prepares a new research agenda. The federal government remains a major source of research funding. There are two major forces currently driving the increases in research funding. First, a general force with an underlying belief that research helps improve economic competitiveness. Second, the force of defined and immediate needs, specifically caused by the Reagan administration's emphasis on increased defense research in the sense of national urgency, and medical research to conquer AIDS.

The question is not so much whether these forces are legitimate, but Do these forces have a long-term philosophical underpinning that is necessary to sustain our society? Often the debate concerning research focuses on the conflicts between basic and applied research or between "pure" research and utilitarian research. These debates for the most part address the wrong issues. A more fruitful approach is an examination of society's research needs on a time continuum. That is, first develop a broad understanding of our nation's short, intermediate, and long-term goals. Second, examine what knowledge is needed to achieve these goals. Third, determine what stages of research are needed to develop this knowledge.

This report, written by Alan Lindsay and Ruth Neumann of Macquarie University in Australia, analyzes the major literature concerning research and focuses on the concept of excellence *and* utility. This conceptual framework helps to produce fourteen recommendations to guide future research development. Higher education has always had finite resources and personnel, but an infinite ability to plan and prioritize its efforts. The underlying philosophy and values that guide this plan will determine much of the future of research. This report helps to develop the conceptual framework that harmonizes the conflicting forces that drive the research effort.

Jonathan D. Fife
Professor and Director
ERIC Clearinghouse on Higher Education
School of Education and Human Development
The George Washignton University

INTRODUCTION

The purposes of university research continually evolve as societies redefine their needs and perspectives. In the processes of judging and directing university research, "excellence" and "utility" have always been central concerns, although their meanings—and the criteria applied in judgments about them—have changed over time. Their relative importance has varied too, with sometimes excellence, sometimes utility, in ascendancy. During some periods in the history of higher education, excellence and utility have been compatible, even harmonious, goals, while in others, they have been in conflict, even contradiction.

Notions of excellence and utility have been instrumental in reshaping and expanding higher education's research role since World War II. During this period, the prevailing notions of excellence and utility have gradually become less harmonious as the pattern of development in higher education has narrowed in meaning, first for excellence and then for utility. The narrowness of the notions of excellence and utility currently holding sway has led to a clash between the dictates of excellence and those of utility. As the difficulty in obtaining research funds has increased, researchers have become frustrated that excellent proposals are not being funded, while governments and industry groups have wanted utility to be given much greater, even dominant, weight in funding decisions. Under these circumstances, utility and excellence have come more and more into conflict. On the one hand, the "ivory-tower" stance of researchers has been criticized, on the other, the instrumentalism of governments and industry (Advisory Board 1987; Australian Science and Technology Council 1987; Brown 1985; *Chronicle of Higher Education* 1985; Elzinga 1985; Lepkowski 1984; Lynton and Elman 1987; Neumann and Lindsay 1987; Smith 1982; Zollinger 1982).

The need is pressing to reverse the growing polarization of viewpoints within the research community that is acting to the detriment of research, universities, and society. An important step toward being able to make an informed judgment about contemporary problems and appropriate responses is to develop an understanding of the relevant historical elements. Often in higher education, and certainly in relation to the role of research, these elements have their origin in the distant past. Later chapters draw upon a broad historical perspective, but an initial appreciation of the dimensions of the current predicament

The need is pressing to reverse the growing polarization of viewpoints within the research community that is acting to the detriment of research, universities, and society.

can be obtained by reviewing the development of higher education's research role in the period following World War II.

The Legacy of Expansion

In broad terms, the university systems of Western nations have followed similar paths since World War II. In the early part of this period, policy on science and policy on higher education developed separately but harmoniously as the postwar faith in both science and higher education was applied under conditions of increasing economic affluence. Both disciplines and institutions proliferated as higher education systems expanded rapidly throughout the 1960s (Best 1988; Slaughter 1988). This expansion was fueled by the imperatives of policy on both science and higher education, each of which was based on a belief in the economic and social benefits of research and an educated work force (Blume 1982; Wittrock 1985b).

In the United States, the spectacular success of the wartime alliance between the federal government and the research system paved the way for the government to become the major source of support for university research. The National Science Foundation and other agencies were created to sponsor this research, and foundations and businesses began to provide more substantial support. A period of unprecedented progress and prosperity followed. This boom resulted not from a single explicit policy but from the fortuitous combination of increasing federal support for research in universities with expanding enrollments and increasing levels of support for higher education generally. Although individual federal departments were essentially "purchasing R&D" rather than "investing in a research system," the overall forms and levels of support did result in the development of a strong university research system (Phillips 1982).

The pace and magnitude of the expansion of higher education were unprecedented, and they changed, quite fundamentally, the nature of higher education, its place in society, and its relationship with government (Kerr 1987). Before World War II, American universities conducted large-scale research in only a few fields—agriculture, medicine, and engineering, for example. For the most part, faculty engaged in research received little outside support and undertook quite heavy teaching loads (Mayhew 1973). Although small by today's standards, the research effort in American higher education reflected a relatively strong orientation, in international terms, toward the problems of society and toward applying the tools of science and technology to the solution of these problems. The relationship between higher education and industry was low key but fruitful. During the postwar boom, this established relationship was eclipsed by the federal government's support for basic scientific research in the national interest and for its own specific needs (Lynton and Elman 1987; Omenn and Prager 1982; Rosenzweig and Turlington 1982). The orientation of the expanding research system was toward basic rather than applied research, reflecting the belief that the essential focus of research should be the systematic and methodical search for new knowledge without any specific potential application in mind. Western governments of the time accepted the argument that such research, while apparently lacking in relevance to society, is the long-term "foundation of both applied research and of development and is therefore quite indispensable to society" (Andren 1982, p. 21). In essence then, this period was one in which the federal government's policy reflected a broad view of utility that encompassed a commitment to excellence in basic research and was directed toward broad national economic and social objectives rather than toward the immediate needs of industry and commerce.

Research under Pressure

After this brief golden age, university research in industrialized countries suffered from a growing reluctance among governments to maintain the range and level of their commitments to funding. In most countries, the spectacular growth in expenditures for research had leveled off by the early 1970s (Organisation for Economic Cooperation and Development 1980). Since then, many Western governments have been steadily reducing the range of disciplines and institutions in which high-level research and teaching is to be maintained. Over the last two decades, commitment to supporting basic research has declined, and governments have progressively moved away from regarding university research as useful in a broad, generalized way and begun to seek utility in the more specific form of immediate technological applications that will bring economic benefits. The rapidly escalating cost of equipment for advanced research has been an important factor in this trend, but the major influences have been the state of national economies and the increased international competition in manufacturing industry (Botkin, Dimancescu, and Stata 1982).

Behind the current emphasis on a narrow form of utility is the urgent need to mobilize the resources of our universities in the struggle with economic and social problems and the quest for technological innovation. In consequence, a worldwide drive has occurred for more productive links between higher education and industry.

[Indeed,] the 1980s may some day be recalled as the decade in which there was the first genuine awareness or appreciation of the increasing interdependence of each nation's business corporations, government agencies, and institutions of higher education (Fincher 1984, p. 10).

Mechanisms for linking universities and industry—and their benefits and problems—have been extensively discussed and summarized in the literature in recent years (see, for example, Baer 1980; Barber 1985; Breslin 1986; Brown 1985; Clarke 1986; Johnson 1984; Tolbert 1985). With its long-standing tradition of service epitomized by the land-grant universities, American higher education is well placed to lead the field in the quest for cooperative links. The contrast between American and British progress in developing these relationships is stark (Shattock 1986).

Some dangers have also been associated with this trend, however. The high-tech connection applies to only a small number of fields, and the funds obtained are for very specific purposes. Consequently, the priorities given to the various fields and disciplines are being reordered, and the balance between "fundamental" and "applied" research is changing. Success of the current strategy involves not only the successful transfer of new knowledge into industry but also the long-term maintenance of scientific preeminence in the field concerned (Press 1982). The mechanisms for effective transfer have been rather neglected in the past, and the risk exists that the transfer of knowledge will now be overemphasized at the expense of investment in basic research. Some faculty also fear that "commercial" attitudes will compromise the established excellence and diversity of research by impairing basic research and the free flow of information and weaken the teaching-research nexus that is widely regarded as an essential ingredient in the extraordinary success of the modern research university (Ben-David 1977; Committee of Vice Chancellors 1986; Geiger 1985b; Muir 1987b; Redner 1987; White 1982).

Certainly, the apparent harmony between research and teaching in universities characteristic of the years of expansion has been replaced as science policy and higher education policy have diverged over the last 15 years, with conflicting demands and growing pressure on the nexus between teaching and research. For some time, many university faculty members in the sciences have been predominantly occupied with graduate education and research (Atelsek and Gomberg 1976; National Commission 1980). An unfortunate consequence has been the creation of a division between undergraduate teaching and research in many universities. In some cases, undergraduate teaching lacks the vitalizing contact with new knowledge, the faculty have become polarized by their different loyalties, and unhealthy conflicts have developed between institutional boards and committees responsible for undergraduate education and those responsible for planning research and for graduate education (Mayhew 1973). The flight from teaching by faculty seeking the status and rewards of research and the neglect of the teaching-research connection have become widespread concerns (Organisation for Economic Cooperation and Development 1981; Redner 1987; Stecklein 1982).

Trends in Funding Research

American higher education research has a long tradition of diverse funding from both public and private sources, although large-scale funding is a relatively recent development (Miller 1970). In 1940, American universities and colleges received only $31 million for scientific research, with 20 percent of it from the federal government. Thirty-five years later, spending for research was a thousand times greater at $3.4 billion, with more than 50 percent coming from the federal government. In constant dollars, these numbers represent a 25-fold increase in the nation's expenditure on university research during the period (Ford Foundation 1977).

With this rate of growth, the United States led the world in the proportion of gross national product devoted to research and development. More recent events give less cause for satisfaction, however. While in the United States the proportion of GNP spent on R&D declined from about 2.8 percent in 1966 to about 2.2 percent in 1978 before recovering to about 2.6 percent in 1984, Japan and West Germany have shown steady increases—from below 2 percent in 1966 to parity with the United States in 1984. In terms of the proportion of GNP de-

voted to nonmilitary R&D, Japan and West Germany are well ahead. Through the 1980s, a marked shift has occurred in the United States toward military research, with almost all the increase going to it. Defense's share of total federal expenditures for R&D is now more than 70 percent, after remaining at a constant 50 percent between 1966 and 1981. And the bulk of the increases in expenditures for defense has been in development, which tends to direct funds away from the universities (Knight 1987).

Much of the data on expenditures for research are unreliable, so caution must be exercised in interpreting differences and trends, especially across nations. A detailed study for the British Advisory Board for the Research Councils of government funding of academic research in six countries (Britain, France, Japan, the Netherlands, the United States, and West Germany) identified four main problems with data from the Organisation for Economic Cooperation and Development (OECD): (1) the lack of comparability among the higher education systems, (2) the methods to estimate expenditures for research within general university funds, (3) the high level of aggregation by field, and (4) the lack of information on the different types of support (Martin and Irvine 1986). The data used provide information with varying degrees of reliability about disciplines and groups of disciplines. Government expenditures on academic research as a percentage of GNP range from 0.5 percent in The Netherlands to 0.37 percent in West Germany to 0.28 percent in France to 0.27 percent in the United States and the United Kingdom to 0.24 percent in Japan. The distribution of funding by discipline reveals considerable differences, with Japan being well ahead in engineering, France in the physical sciences, and the United States in the life sciences. The United States devotes the smallest proportion to the arts and humanities, with a figure less than half that of the other countries.

Overall, expenditures on basic research in American higher education declined throughout the early 1970s but have grown steadily over the last decade, with the biggest proportional increase in funds coming from industry. While the proportion of funding for basic research allocated to the universities has remained at about 50 percent, the proportion financed by the federal government has declined from 77 percent to 67 percent during this period, with the largest drop occurring with the advent of the Reagan administration ("Academic R&D" 1982; Knight 1987).

Like business, the Department of Defense (DOD) sharply increased its funding for university research in the 1980s. In the first half of the decade, DOD funding increased by 89 percent, while National Science Foundation (NSF) support grew by only 51 percent. The budget for FY 1987, however, contained large increases for the NSF, and for the National Institutes of Health, achieved by strong lobbying by researchers (Slaughter 1988).

The increasing militarization of R&D under the Reagan administration has led to an emphasis on the physical sciences. Between 1981 and 1984, federal support for university mathematical and physical sciences experienced real growth of 4.2 percent per year, in contrast to about 1 percent in engineering and the life sciences and against an overall growth rate for university basic research of 1.2 percent. Environmental research declined about 1 percent, social science research about 10 percent per year (Knight 1987, p. 7). Overall, federal spending for academic research has been experiencing only modest growth, which has been concentrated in the mathematical and physical sciences and selected areas of engineering, while support in many other disciplines is declining.

As the largest defense program, the Strategic Defense Initiative (SDI) has been a significant part of this trend. With university contracts exceeding $200 million in 1986, SDI sponsorship matched that of the National Aeronautics and Space Administration and reached about a quarter of that provided by the NSF. In terms of total expenditures, SDI outstripped the NSF with a budget of $3.5 billion in FY 1987. SDI has provided a significant and growing fraction of university funding for R&D. The program has the potential to affect the way university research is performed through its emphasis on mission-oriented research and its restrictions on the flow of information. With foreign graduate students comprising one-third to one-half of many science and engineering departments (Knight 1987), the military significance of research work has important ramifications for teaching as well.

The surge of industrial and military interest in university biotechnology also raises fundamental concerns. A particular danger in this instance is the compromising of academic judgments and the peer review process by the commercial interests, possibly undisclosed, of faculty involved in the review of grant applications (Wofsy 1986).

Clearly, with the increasing influence on university research from both the Pentagon and industry, the issues of academic freedom, the restriction of knowledge, and political manipulation of the university require careful consideration and the introduction of appropriate safeguards (Bok 1982; Knight 1987; Slaughter 1988).

Concerns about Current Directions in Policy

The drive to ensure that university research has more immediate utility to economic goals has generally been one element in a broader strategy among Western governments. The latest OECD report shows that this strategy has involved attempts to achieve tighter control of research policy and funding, greater concentration of research effort, reductions in the proportion of faculty who engage in research, and reductions in overall expenditures on research (OECD 1987). Even in the United States, where policy has been decentralized, almost laissez-faire, in contrast to the more interventionist approaches of Western European countries, a more managerial approach is developing (Best 1988; Brickman 1985; Elzinga 1985).

These policies have in part been adopted because of their appeal as easy solutions to very deep-seated and complex problems. Their full effects are not yet clear, but the forces involved are clearly powerful enough to alter the basic nature of universities and, in particular, the nature of their research role. University research, especially in the high-cost fields, has gradually changed under the pressures of the last decade, becoming increasingly divorced from the teaching function as it has become associated with large team projects and special research units. Given the extent of obsolescent equipment, the changes may be desirable, even inevitable, for some fields, but they do carry potential dangers that have not received sufficient consideration—possible reductions in the overall level of research, increased aversion to taking risks, bureaucratization of the funding process, overemphasis on short-term applied research goals at the expense of more fundamental research and on science and technology at the expense of the social sciences and humanities.

Fields that do not use traditional research paradigms may also be disadvantaged. The term "research" is used in many different ways, from the narrow view of research as relating only to laboratory-based scientific experiments to the broader view that encompasses such scholarly activities as observation, chronicling, critical evaluation, construction of theories, and inegration. The current trend favors the hard sciences and conservative notions of research.

University research is being made to serve an ever-growing variety of purposes, and the total set of demands imposed on universities becomes ever more onerous and contradictory. The president of Stanford University has described the problems facing the modern research university: secrecy in research, the ethics and economics of proprietary knowledge generated in the university, faculty conflicts of interest, the place of the humanities in a society driven by technology, and the decline in government support for academic research (Kennedy 1982). The decline of government funding in areas other than defense and the increase in industry's support for fundamental research have contributed to a blurring of the notions of how basic and applied research should be undertaken. The conflicts of interest arise from the university's role of social critic clashing with the economic and commercial character of the modern research university.

These increased demands are being placed on universities at the time when their capacity to respond has been reduced by widespread obsolescence in equipment and rigidities in staffing. Western governments are extending their interest from issues of resources and efficiency, however, to include more basic questions of purpose and outcome (OECD 1981, 1982, 1987). Amid strong criticism of the current organization and orientation of university research, questions are being asked about the overall amount of research needed by society, the mix of pure and applied research, the balance of effort across fields, the levels of concentration appropriate for research in the various fields, and the best means of coordination, control, and funding. These issues are fundamental and the decisions made will directly affect the future nature of university research and teaching. Before the urgency of the situation leads to the widespread adoption of easy solutions, a pressing need exists for more detailed consideration of the issues, broader debate about needs and priorities, and more rigorous inquiry into the performance of the research system and the potential benefits of the new policies. Key topics include the changes in the notion of research, its purposes and functions, selectivity and concentration, relationships with government and industry, social responsibility, and sources of and mechanisms for funding.

This study addresses issues at the heart of the present predicament. Recent policies and practices have developed in such a way that the two traditional driving forces in American higher education—the quest for utility and the pursuit of excellence—tend to be at odds with each other. The economic and social problems currently confronting all Western societies are long-term ones that will continue well into the 1990s, and so a reemphasis on the utility of university research is both desirable and inevitable. The challenge to higher education is to bring the goals of excellence and utility into harmony—to reincorporate utility as a fundamental concern without compromising the pursuit of excellence.

Bringing excellence and utility into harmony again is a formidable challenge, and it is complicated by the complex nature of universities themselves. Universities are among the most enduring institutions in Western society. Their culture is one in which new ideas and structures overlay rather than replace existing ones. Hence, alongside contemporary notions and forces are the residual but still powerful echoes of the past (Brubacher 1977; Muir 1987a). Consequently, when excellence and utility are discussed in higher education, multiple meanings operate simultaneously. Finding these meanings is not a simple task, but it is an essential one if we are to understand current events and influence future developments.

This study is designed to contribute to this process. It examines the recent trends in higher education's research role against a backdrop of centuries of development. Its focus is on the evolution of the notions of excellence and utility that have guided research policy and funding. Proposals for harmonizing excellence and utility are examined and the implications for future research policy and management discussed. Specific recommendations are directed to four broad constituencies in higher education: faculty in the various disciplines, institutional leaders and administrators, policy makers, and sponsors and users of research. The issues addressed are dealt with both at the general level and in relation to the broad fields of the natural sciences, the social sciences, and the humanities. Attention is also given to the pressures that the current events and changes are exerting on the role of teaching and the opportunities they present, with particular consideration of the implications for doctoral education.

The approach adopted has three distinctive features. First, university research is reviewed in its international context, referring to experiences in OECD countries where relevant. The research community has an international character, and, while the center of gravity of science moved decisively from Europe to the United States after World War II, an international perspective can still do much to illuminate the topic. The problems facing American universities have much in common with those in other Western countries, although distinct solutions must be sought for every setting.

Second, this study avoids treating "science" policy and "research" policy as identical to the exclusion of the special needs and character of research in the social sciences and humanities. All too frequently, discussions of research policy are actually discussions of science policy, and even within science, it tends to be assumed that uniform policies are applicable across all fields. The differences between fields may be substantial, however, and quite often different policies are warranted. For example, the level of concentration of research necessary for efficient use of resources varies considerably by field. Some fields in the natural sciences, high-energy physics, for example, require intensive concentration, while others and most social sciences benefit from broad, diverse, small-scale approaches.

Third, the study contributes to connecting more closely the scholarly literature on the nature of research, particularly scientific research, and the literature in the field of higher education. These two bodies of literature have tended to develop in isolation from each other and would benefit from more interchange of ideas and perspectives (Schwartzman 1984; Wittrock 1985a).

EXCELLENCE AND UTILITY:
A First Encounter

Excellence is "a curiously powerful word—a word about which people [feel] strongly and deeply" (Gardner 1961, p. xii). It has been the subject of many books, both in education (for example, Astin 1985; Buxton and Prichard 1975; Gardner 1961; Leverhulme Report 1983) and in other fields (for example, Peters and Waterman 1982). Utility too has been an important concern (see, for example, Johnson 1984; Lynton and Elman 1987).

Excellence has at times been used to justify the neglect of social responsibilities.

Both excellence and utility are pivotal concepts in contemporary research policy. Both terms have multiple meanings, which influence thought about policy. To understand their explanatory power and their role in current events and then to use this knowledge in influencing future developments, we must study the prominent part that notions of "excellence" and "utility" have played in shaping higher education throughout its history and the central place they hold in the philosophies that justify our view of higher education. This chapter provides a first encounter with the notions in simple terms and with only a brief incursion into the complexities of their contextual meanings, which will emerge in later chapters.

At first sight, "excellence" and "utility" seem to be fairly straightforward terms. Excellence denotes superlative performance, superior merit, or a state of preeminence. To excel at something is to do well or even to outdo all others. The notion of excellence thus refers to the quality or caliber of a performance's being superb or brilliant in some absolute sense or being outstanding or superior relative to others. The term "utility" refers to usefulness—the capacity to yield benefits or satisfy wants. To have utility means to be suitable for some purpose. The term is used to distinguish the property of practical or material usefulness from properties like truth or beauty.

Each term refers to a state or attribute of some object or activity, and each also has connotations that complicate its meaning in both general and educational uses. Excellence tends to be thought of as an entity or a goal in its own right rather than as a level of achievement in some activity. In academe, this thinking is seen in the expression "the pursuit of excellence," which often appears in the exhortative literature on goals virtually as an end in itself and without sufficient specification of the endeavor in which excellence is sought. While "the pursuit of excellence" indicates that striving to do as well as possible is being given a high priority, excellence cannot be pursued in

---

the abstract. Excellence per se does not exist. The tendency to focus on the act of striving to excel rather than on the activity in which excellence is sought, however, makes the pursuit of excellence to some degree a self-justifying activity. Achieving excellence is a perennial human aspiration, and striving to excel is regarded as virtuous or valuable independently to some extent of the value of the goal sought.

These connotations of excellence can be traced to the thought of classical Greece. Homer derived the word *areté* from Ares, the Greek deification of the warlike spirit, and used it to designate the qualities of manhood, valor, and nobility. Socrates and Plato extended the term to include moral and intellectual qualities, and by the time of Aristotle, excellence was defined as the conjunction of virtue and knowledge. To be excellent was to have the capacity for excellence and to strive to attain it. Such attainment was true virtue (Bowen 1978). Excellence thus became identified with three interrelated conditions: quality of mind, performance at a high standard, and seriousness of purpose. Through the idea of "quality of mind," excellence became regarded as a human characteristic, inferred from specific activities or performances but to some extent stable and consistent and thus generalizable. The concern with seriousness of purpose eliminates trivial activities and attitudes by requiring a disposition toward respecting and striving for the highest standards (Brown 1978).

Similarly, the notion of utility is a fundamental one of some complexity. Utility has been equated with value, where value is defined solely by the object's or activity's instrumental use or function in human experience or progress. Even more narrowly, utility can be equated with value as determined by exchange or sale rather than with value as determined by the accrued or potential benefits of possession or use. A market-price mechanism is not always the only, or even the best, way of determining value, however. The outputs of teaching and research in higher education cannot be readily defined—let alone have their value captured by market prices (Bowen 1977; Creswell 1985; Lindsay 1982). For example, some value the national research effort only for its contributions to economic prosperity and the standard of living. Others see intellectual or aesthetic value in addition to the value residing in these instrumental uses.

Changing Notions of Excellence and Utility

Even this simple discussion of meaning demonstrates the importance of context in determining meaning. In higher education, the notions of excellence and utility have particular meanings and important uses. Throughout the history of higher education, notions of excellence and utility have influenced its nature and form. The notions themselves have changed in meaning over time, however, and their level of influence in the university culture has waxed and waned. For example, pursuing and valuing excellence are now well established as core values. Indeed, the reverence for excellence, now hallowed by tradition, has come to obscure its meaning, so that the pursuit of excellence has been the justification for faculty's self-indulgence as well as for outstanding achievement or service to society. In any event, the current preeminence of excellence dates only from the 19th century, with von Humboldt's reforms in Germany, the influence of the German model on American universities through the example of the Johns Hopkins University, and the reform of Oxford and Cambridge. This emphasis on excellence came after a long period of complacent mediocrity.

At the most general level, excellence in higher education refers to achieving high quality, so that concepts of excellence and quality are essentially the same. Six views of institutional quality or excellence have been identified (Astin 1980, 1985). The first is the *mystical* or *nihilistic view*, in which quality simply cannot be defined because institutions are just too complex and their products too intangible for capture by measurement or judgment. The *reputational view* relies on the consensus of opinion about an institution's ranking in prestige. Those seeking a more direct measurement favor the *resources view*, which links quality to the level of resources enjoyed. The *outcomes view* provides a more sophisticated but less operationally feasible approach. These last three notions are closely related: Quality of outcome is related to quality of input, and reputation reflects both. A fifth view defines quality or excellence in terms of an institution's *content* in relation to the traditional liberal arts curriculum of humanities, social sciences, and natural sciences. The sixth approach, the *value-added* or *talent development view,* focuses on the contribution or impact of the institution rather than merely on its current ability to attract high-quality students and resources.

Despite some clarification of the concept, attempts to measure quality have nevertheless been limited in success (Creswell 1985; Kruh 1982; Lawrence and Green 1980). Quality like excellence remains an elusive, intangible attribute. Hence, the mystical view of quality and excellence is widespread in higher education and underlies the universal belief in peer review as the appropriate procedure for assessment.

Universities have also shown a remarkable ability to maintain their utility to society. By developing in response to the changing needs of society, universities have endured as social institutions. While utility has always been important, what is considered useful has undergone many revisions. At times, the notion of utility has been used to justify pure research on the grounds of its intellectual value and overall long-term benefits to society—at other times to denigrate it on the grounds of its irrelevance to society's problems. For centuries, utility resided in mastery of the prevailing religious dogma and systems of thought before the emphasis shifted to open inquiry and independent thought (Stone 1983). Thus, the forms of knowledge and skill considered relevant and useful for later life change, but the goal of utility endures. At the present time, the notion of utility has become clouded by the discourse within the higher education culture. As well as serving the cause of both pure and applied research, utility has been invoked to support opposing sides in the debate about the relative merits and desirable mix of general liberal education and specialized vocational education. The champions of the former see education's utility in its fostering of understanding, analytical ability, flexibility, and adaptability; the proponents of the latter see utility in terms of direct and immediate benefits for specific job situations. In the 1960s, concern for utility surfaced in the guise of calls for relevance, although the criteria for relevance were not clarified.

Philosophical Justifications of Higher Education
Just how fundamental a place excellence and utility occupy in higher education can be seen by examining the philosophies legitimating higher education. Two dominant philosophies in higher education have been identified—the epistemological and the political (Brubacher 1977, pp. 12–25). The abstract, detached notion of excellence so frequently found in the literature on higher education is grounded in the epistemological philosophy, which regards the quest for knowledge as a self-legitimating activity. Linking this quest with a devotion to truth, theoretical simplicity, explanatory power, conceptual

legance, and logical coherence describes the scholar's notion f the pursuit of excellence. In the political philosophy, the stification for the pursuit of knowledge is not merely curisity but its significance for society, that is, utility. The same nderlying concepts have been labeled the "autonomous" and he "service" traditions, with the former pursuing excellence n its self-justifying sense and the latter seeking utility (Buress 1978). In the early years of the nation, the education of rofessionals was the main function of higher education, and o its legitimation was largely political. With the founding of ohns Hopkins University, the epistemological justification of he German model became important and flourished alongside he political one. The Wisconsin model combined the two nto the American model of pure research in the service of he nation.

Understanding and attempting to solve the complex problems of society have increasingly involved the resources of the niversities. Nevertheless, for some faculty a basic lack of armony exists between the epistemological and political justiications, which usually leads them to advocate choosing the bjectivity and detachment of the former. Others attack the asic notion of objectivity, arguing that knowledge is power nd "as negotiable as gold" (Brubacher 1977, p. 19). Curently, the two justifications exist side by side in the pluralistic ulture of American higher education, sometimes in conflict, ometimes at least in apparent harmony.

Although the higher education culture is continually being modified by contemporary social, political, and economic orces, some elements of it embody the traditions accumulated ver many centuries. Consequently, institutional policies and aculty behavior reflect not only rational analysis of the current ituation and its imperatives but also a traditional culture of onsiderable complexity, which provides enduring beliefs, vales, and perspectives. They are acquired from mentors and nore senior colleagues during the socialization process associted with professional training as academics (Muir 1987a; Tierey 1988).

The higher education culture has both explicit and implicit imensions. At the explicit or conscious level, the culture is ubject to scrutiny and change in response to current pressures nd events. Many powerful features of the higher education ulture are implicit, however. Higher education is characterized y ambiguous and conflicting goals and poorly understood processes (Cohen and March 1974), and much of its operating logic is consequently provided by traditional values and modes of behavior acquired unconsciously through the apprenticeship of Ph.D. training. The implicit level of the higher education culture reflects the long history of higher education and embodies the accumulation and overlay of past values and beliefs. Although present universities are in a number of ways radically different from those of 800, 300, or even 100 years ago, some important aspects have endured; that is, a continuity exists of past and present quite distinctive among the institutions of Western society. Thus, the conditions and beliefs of the past sometimes influence academic judgments as much or more than rational analysis of the current situation (Muir 1987a, pp. 7–17).

It is for this reason that this study seeks to develop an understanding of the historical context in which excellence and utility have evolved and exerted their influence on the shape of higher education. Support for a contextual approach is provided by the recent research on academic culture (Becher 1981; Dill 1982a, 1982b; Muir 1987a). Over time, the interplay of excellence and utility within the higher education culture has produced various and even conflicting meanings. Excellence has at times been used to justify the neglect of social responsibilities and at others the pursuit of fundamentally important knowledge in the face of government apathy or opposition. Similarly, utility has been used both to legitimate pure research and to denigrate it. The following sections explore in greater detail these many faces of excellence and utility in higher education.

EXCELLENCE AND UTILITY IN
HISTORICAL PERSPECTIVE

This section provides a brief historical overview of the development of higher education from the Middle Ages to the present to show how excellence and utility in various forms have always been embodied in the contemporary views about the nature and purposes of higher education. It describes the context and furnishes the perspective for the subsequent examination of the role of research in higher education and the connections between teaching and research.

The functions of higher education and our concepts of its purposes have evolved over the long period of the existence of universities. They have been shaped by a range of influences— the prevailing modes of thought and values, dominant and distinguished individuals, economic conditions, the social context of the particular country. In reflecting on the purposes and functions of higher education, two major eras can be discerned, with possibly a third taking shape (Ben-David 1977; Kerr 1972).

To be accepted as subjects worthy of study in a university, the sciences had to justify themselves in terms of their instrinsic value and shed their 18th century emphasis on utility.

The Medieval University: Excellence and
Utility in Enlightenment

The first era is that of the medieval university, an era that lasted until approximately 1800, when the period of the modern university (the university as we know it today) began. The origins of the medieval university are somewhat obscure. It was not a planned institution but rather a spontaneous event when scholars and students collected together in major towns. This association was usually connected with a cathedral or a famous teacher, and the reason for grouping together into a community of scholars was the need for protection from exploitation by the townspeople. The purpose of these communities of scholars was to study, learn, and teach the knowledge inherited from the great ancient civilizations. The prime function was thus the preservation and transmission of this knowledge, which consisted predominantly of Aristotelian and theological dogmas and was believed to represent the totality of knowledge. A second function arose, the examining of candidates to enable them to embark upon a clerical or civil service career, and other candidates were examined and licensed to teach in the growing academic community. Thus, the medieval university was primarily a teaching institution committed to the preservation and transmission of knowledge. Much of our current conception of scholarship dates back to this tradition. Of key importance in understanding the medieval university is to appreciate that, in a continuous tradition from classical times, the essential approach to learning was:

> . . .*sheer intellection, the Greek notion of "noesis": the ability of the mind to make connections and to achieve understanding, by pure intuitive grasp, resulting thereby in the supreme state of "enlightenment"* (Bowen 1978, p. 31).

In such a setting, the cardinal virtue of excellence in the classical sense was readily accepted. Excellence in the form of intellectual virtuosity was achieved by the exercise, through logic, of the individual's innate endowment of intuitive noetic skill. In the medieval societies that contained these universities, mastery of the prevailing religious dogma and systems of thought was of considerable utility. It provided entry into clerical and administrative careers, which were a major means of acquiring power for those not born to it.

This approach to learning came under serious attack during the 15th and 16th centuries, however. Seminal thinkers like Francis Bacon developed the doctrine of empiricism, which became the means of breaking the shackles of Aristotelian thought and method (West 1965). Significantly, empiricism was not adopted and developed by the universities, which remained secure in their comfortable orthodoxy, but by the learned and scientific academies, such as the Royal Society founded in 1660. The universities for the most part degenerated to the periphery of intellectual and scientific development, although their prestige ensured their survival and continuing power. Responding to the utility of the "new" knowledge and methods, alternative institutions developed to cater to the needs not being met by the universities (Bowen 1978).

The Modern University: Excellence and Utility in Research
The universities mostly remained outside the mainstream of intellectual development until the 19th century, when a tide of reform overtook them. Although many of the basic features of our present universities can be traced back to the Middle Ages, our current concept of higher education stems primarily from the reforms of late 18th and early 19th century German universities. These reforms were based on an acceptance of the view that the purpose of higher education was to advance as well as to preserve and transmit knowledge. The current view of research as a prestigious and self-justifying activity was born

with these reforms, which incorporated empiricism into the university and harmonized it with the classical tradition. The emphasis in the German universities on the advancement of knowledge for its own sake with no immediate concern for practical application distanced the notion of research from the practical and rather technical focus of the scientific academies and enabled the classical notion of excellence to be retained, albeit with some reformulation.

The notion that "new" knowledge existed, not only that of the ancient scholars, revolutionized the academic world. It meant that institutions of higher education should be involved in research as well as teaching. The major differences between universities before the 19th century and those after were their essentially very different assumptions about the nature of knowledge, its organization, its method of advancement, and its relationship with teaching (Turner 1974). As a consequence, the activities of universities were necessarily based on specialized science and scholarship. The proper scope of study was broadened to include not only the sciences and the basic arts but also those professional studies based on basic science as well as those based on an intellectual tradition, such as law or theology (Ben-David 1977). With the introduction of research, disciplines emerged and proliferated, leading to disciplinary values' coming in contact and at times conflict with collegiate values, which emphasized teaching.

The key figure in the 19th century reforms of the German universities was Wilhelm von Humboldt, who espoused what Turner (1971) has termed the *Wissenschaftsideologie*, or "ideology of knowledge." This ideology maintained that *Wissenschaft*, which is translated as "knowledge" or "science" used in its broadest sense, was a pure, unified whole. It embodied a dynamic concept of learning, emphasized creativity, and stressed the importance of knowledge for the moral development of the individual and the nation. A group of influential thinkers of the time, including the philosopher Johann Gottlieb Fichte, expounded these ideas. According to von Humboldt:

Universities should view knowledge as incomplete and so subject to discovery, although full or final knowledge could never be attained. Further, knowledge was pure and was to be found deep within the self. It could not be gained merely by the extensive collection of facts. Only knowledge that came from, and could be developed within, the self formed one's character, and it was character and the manner of behaving that was important for the state and for humanity, not merely knowledge and eloquence (Scurla 1984, p. 345, summary translation from the German by R. Neumann).

The reforms von Humboldt put into practice in his short but influential period as minister for education revolutionized higher education around the world. The ideology, a strong reaction to the utilitarian mode of thinking of the Enlightenment:

. . .created a new image of the scholar as an individual of moral insight and courage, simultaneously aware of his radical personal freedom and his responsibilities to the state (Turner 1971, p. 141).

It was believed that true knowledge involved an insight into the unity of all knowledge and that the universities exemplified this ideal of knowledge. A core belief was the unity of research and teaching—and hence of researcher and teacher. Research and scholarship were seen as dynamic, creative activities fundamental to teaching. It was argued that only what the teacher-scholar had gained as a result of creative research was truly knowledge and thus the only teaching and knowledge befitting a university and university study.

Accompanying this "research revolution" were the concepts of *Lehrfreit* and *Lernfreiheit*, that is, the academic's freedom to teach what he considered to be the appropriate knowledge and the student's freedom to decide on the course of study to undertake. These two concepts form the basis of our current understanding of academic freedom. The freedom of research and teaching together with the unity of research and teaching provide the foundation of the relationship between the university and the state. Thus, the important legacies for higher education from von Humboldt's reforms are the conviction that a university academic should actively pursue the advancement of knowledge in his or her field, the principle of the interconnection and unity of this advanced knowledge with the function of teaching, and the formalization of academic freedom.

Although predicated on excellence rather than on utility, the German university reforms were of great utility for the nation. The *Wissenschaftsideologie* saw universities as the symbol of German cultural unity that embodied the ideal of *Wissenschaft* and combined the mission of universities with German patriotic sentiment while simultaneously connecting it to German philosophical and scholarly thought. The long-term benefits through the development of German science were immense, but short-term benefits accrued as well. The system of higher education established by von Humboldt came at the time of Prussia's humiliation in war with France. The aim was to create a system of higher learning that would be superior to that of the French. The real political purpose of the pursuit of excellence was the development of national identity—hence, the basic motive of utility in the emphasis on excellence.

The successful practice of these philosophies in German universities led to their enthusiastic adoption by most other European countries and the United States, although modifications and variations naturally arose. England eventually adopted elements of the new model, but a belief in the supremacy of the elite teaching function of the university in molding the cultivated gentleman held sway for many years—and indeed still exerts a strong influence today. The most influential English thinker in the 19th century was Cardinal Newman, whose views on the purposes of universities were developed during his long period at Oxford and formalized in a series of discourses on the founding of the Catholic university at Dublin.

Like von Humboldt's, Newman's ideas represent something of a return to the philosophy of Aristotle in reaction to the more utilitarian philosophy of the 18th century. In Newman's view, the purpose of a university is the pursuit of truth and intellectual excellence, through which occurs the cultivation of gentlemen. Newman maintained that through a liberal education "a habit of mind is formed [that] lasts through life, of which the attributes are freedom, equitableness, calmness, moderation, and wisdom. . ." (Newman 1960, p. 76). By a liberal education, Newman referred to "simply the cultivation of the intellect, as such, and its object is nothing more or less than intellectual excellence" (Newman 1960, p. 92). He differentiated such education from professional and mechanical learning, which has as its goal financial utility and is therefore not the appropriate function of a university. Newman justified the utility of a university education in Aristotelian terms: The pursuit of intellectual excellence through a liberal education has intrinsic value. As such, liberal education is on a level distinct from other pursuits, such as wealth, power, or honor (Newman 1960, p. 82).

While Newman decried considerations of financial utility in a

university's goals, he seemed to have no difficulty in reconciling his emphasis on the intrinsic value of intellectual excellence and a liberal education with their underlying utility to the upper class and the Catholic church. Additionally, although he regarded the purpose of a university as concern with teaching and education and not with research, Newman, when rector at the Catholic University in Dublin, found that in practice the results from and importance of research needed to be taken into account (Ward 1915, p. x).

The German model was enthusiastically embraced in the United States but was gradually modified in accord with the more utilitarian American attitude toward higher education (Ashby 1967; Veysey 1965). The foundation of Johns Hopkins University was a direct emulation of the German ideology of higher education. As had been the pattern with the establishment of the University of Berlin, the initial aim was to bring to Johns Hopkins the ablest minds and to create a university with a national and even international reputation (Brubacher and Rudy 1968). Johns Hopkins became the first graduate school and model for Harvard and many others in the United States. Like the German model on which it was based, the establishment of Johns Hopkins had an underlying political goal of utility.

Both Veblen and Flexner, writing in the first half of the 20th century, reaffirmed the German model's notions of the purity of research and knowledge for the sake of knowledge. For Veblen, it was the pursuit of knowledge for its own sake and not for any utilitarian purpose that distinguished universities from other institutions. Teaching served the purpose of facilitating the pursuit of new knowledge and was appropriate only for the training of the next generation of researchers and scholars (Veblen 1969). Flexner considered that higher education had four main functions:

> . . .the conservation of knowledge and ideas; the interpretation of knowledge and ideas; the search for truth; [and] the training of students who will practise and "carry on" (Flexner 1967, p. 22).

It was the nature of the university to be actively engaged in investigation and contemplation as the means of pursuing its main aim: to advance knowledge at the highest possible level.

Today, arguments stressing the importance and value of pure research over that of applied research follow in this tradition.

Development of the Role of Service

The land-grant university was a major 19th century American innovation that reasserted the importance of utility. The land-grant colleges were established alongside the graduate schools but with a different philosophical basis that underpinned their major contribution to American economic development (Brubacher and Rudy 1968, p. 234). Their purpose was to provide mass education—in contrast to the elitism of the private universities—to pursue relevance by generating new knowledge within a framework where every area was a legitimate subject of inquiry, and to apply that knowledge to the problems of society. The institutional mission was to address the problems of society and to apply the tools of science and technology to the solution of those problems. Thus, while (according to Newman) the purpose of higher education was to learn from the classics the values and morals that would be of use to a gentleman throughout his life, the development of the service tradition in the United States emphasized the idea of the utility of higher education to all of society—hence, the familiar tripartite mission of teaching, research, and service.

Basic to the land-grant institutions' (and later the multiversities') notion is the view that any topic of importance or relevance to the community is suitable for university study. The classical notion of excellence, which refers to intellectual excellence and a seriousness of purpose, had tended to restrict the curriculum of universities to subjects judged to be "worthy" of study. Over time, the trend has been for this range of subjects to be gradually expanded. Perceptions of worth are also subject to continual change, and this century has seen a rapid increase in the number of areas considered appropriate for university study. Appropriate subjects have evolved from medieval times, when only those subjects embodying the knowledge of the ancient scholars were perceived as useful for the undertaking of clerical and public service professions. During the 17th and 18th centuries, it was argued that worth lay in subjects that developed and cultivated the mind. During the 19th century and into the 20th, a subject worthy of university study had not only to cultivate the mind but also to have an intrinsic value not associated with earning a living.

To be accepted as subjects worthy of study in a university,

the sciences had to justify themselves in terms of their intrinsic value and shed their 18th century emphasis on utility (Turner 1971, p. 152). As a consequence, scientists adopted the terminology of humanists and philosophers, arguing that the study of the sciences also trained the intellect and developed the individual morally and ethically. In the early 19th century, the status of the sciences was low in German universities because they were still seen as maintaining their 18th century emphasis on utility. Thus, to gain prestige and to be accepted into universities as subjects worthy of higher study, the sciences had to be convincingly presented, not merely in utilitarian terms, but in terms of providing training for the mind and of being worthy of study in their own right. Just as in the humanities, independent scientific research served society by contributing to the store of knowledge, in addition to contributing to the development of the individual.

By the late 19th century, "utilitarian" subjects like engineering formed part of university study, but their acceptance was hard won. At times, debate over the appropriateness of professional disciplines in universities has been intense. From the earliest times, disciplines like law, theology, and medicine were studied in universities, preparing students for future professional and administrative careers. The orientation of the higher learning and study was thus primarily utilitarian. With the emphasis on the pursuit of pure learning and pure knowledge in the 19th century German university, many believed the professions and any other areas involving applied research were more suited to an academy or research institute (see, for example, Veblen 1969). Hence, applied, utilitarian forms of knowledge were not considered worthy of university study. In England, under Newman's influence, a similar view held that professional education did not belong in a university, although the reason in this instance was the belief that professional education did not form part of a gentleman's education. In the United States, the land-grant institutions, established to serve society by relating knowledge from higher education to practical social and economic problems, paved the way for the incorporation of a wide array of subjects into the higher education curriculum as appropriate and useful for study and research.

These debates about the range of subjects appropriate for university study are most intense in higher education systems that are less broadly based than the American, but the issues gain prominence everywhere from time to time, either as expressions of intellectual snobbery or more basic concerns with dilution of quality and fragmentation of mission. One view decries "the prostitution of research" by the choice of unworthy or trivial subjects, while another decries elitism and extols the greater relevance of a mission to generate new knowledge and apply it to the problems of society within a framework where every area is a legitimate subject of enquiry (Schuh 1986). The debate about the appropriateness of professional studies in higher education is flawed, however, as history has demonstrated that both pure and professional research thrive most productively when they are conducted jointly (Brubacher 1977, p. 23). Thus, excellence and utility are mutually beneficial.

Nevertheless, these different notions of excellence and utility continue to compete. In teaching, they contend in the elite versus the mass approach. For some, excellence can be achieved only through the elite approach, while others see excellence in promoting access and success in value-added terms. In research, the pure orientation with its long-term benefits and the prestige of pursuing excellence in the classical tradition contends with the applied orientation with its more immediate economic returns and excellence through service to society. Gradually, in the conflict of these different notions—Newman's, which stressed the usefulness of higher education to the upper class, and the land-grant universities', which emphasized the usefulness of higher education to all people and hence to society at large—the broader notion has gained the ascendancy, especially in the United States.

From this vein of democracy in education, with its more elastic views of what was appropriate for university study, grew the notion of the "multiversity," a term popularized by Kerr to describe the movement from a single, unifying goal to a multiplicity of goals. "Multiversity" refers to the modern university as a:

. . . "pluralistic" institution—pluralistic in several senses: in having several purposes, not one; in having several centers of power, not one; in serving several clienteles, not one (Kerr 1972, p. 136).

In his description and analysis of the modern university in American society, Kerr saw the purpose and function of higher education as being far more diverse than did earlier writers.

Flexner, and before him Newman, Kerr argues, were writing at the end of their particular era of the university and instead of philosophizing on what universities should be like, they were in fact exalting an era that was rapidly passing. The ideals proclaimed by Newman, Veblen, Flexner, and others still have their proponents, but these ideals have become incorporated in the multiple purposes and functions that have been added to the traditional ones of teaching and research. This process has been accelerated by the increasing government intrusion into higher education since World War II. As a result of these developments, higher education has "no peers in all history among institutions of higher learning in serving so many of the segments of an advancing civilization" (Kerr 1972, p. 45).

In moving from the periphery of society to occupying a far more central position, the university has adopted additional functions (Kerr 1987). Thus, added to the purposes of preserving, transmitting, and advancing knowledge through teaching and research are the purposes of producing an egalitarian society and advancing the nation through greater access to and participation in education and its rewards. The concept of the multiversity tries to accommodate the many and sometimes conflicting roles and functions of higher education—and with them the alternative and contending notions of excellence and utility. For example, four purposes have been distinguished in the service role alone: producing ideas of value, social criticism, social problem solving, and social action (Crosson 1983). With the complex relationships universities now have with their societies, conflicts can readily arise. For example, the universities' role in providing disinterested scientific advice is increasingly jeopardized by faculty commercial interests and involvement in social action.

Not surprisingly, one result of this pluralism has been a loss of direction, and higher education is consequently experiencing a time of confusion and even crisis of identity (Bok 1982; OECD 1987; Schuh 1986; Scott 1984).

The philosophical tradition to which von Humboldt, Newman, Veblen, and Flexner belonged stemmed from the ideas of classical Greek philosophy. This philosophy provided a view of the world and man's place in it. The tradition also advocated the importance of self-development and pursuing "the truth" and provided the foundations for the moral development deemed necessary for humane learning. It is the absence of this classical philosophy in modern universities and their espousal of the philosophy of relativism that is at the heart of the current confusion and crisis within higher education and within society as a whole (Bloom 1987). Classical philosophy is premised on the central belief that good (or truth) can be attained through knowledge and reason (Bloom 1987); however, the doctrine of relativism at the center of teaching in humanities and the social sciences in universities maintains that knowledge shows that there are many truths—or no one truth—with one value or belief being as good and as valid as another. As a result, there is no goal to strive for, and apathy, indifference, and a loss of direction are the end products. Thus, the malaise in higher education and the community's loss of faith in it are not the result of:

> . . .bad administrators, weakness of will, lack of discipline, lack of money, insufficient attention to the three R's, or any of the other common explanations that indicate things will be set aright if we professors would just pull up our socks. . . .To find out why we have fallen on hard times, we must recognize that the foundations of the university have become extremely doubtful to the highest intelligences (Bloom 1987, p. 312).

THE ROLE OF RESEARCH IN HIGHER EDUCATION

It is virtually impossible to imagine present universities without research, and it is easy to forget that our notion of research and its acceptance as an appropriate activity for higher education derive from its relatively recent introduction and development in German, American, and British universities during the 19th century. In fact, research is now such an integral part of universities that the nature and division of academic work reflect its importance, and the organization of universities provides the framework for its productive existence. The major function of a university is the preservation, transmission, and advancement of knowledge, a function that finds its expression in the nature and organization of academic work. Research is concerned with the preservation and advancement of knowledge, teaching with the preservation and transmission of knowledge. Particularly in the United States, the role of service is concerned with the transmission of knowledge through its application. The organization of universities into departments (according to the British and American models) and chairs (according to the European (German) model) provides the structural framework for academic work to be pursued.

Notwithstanding the universal acceptance of the role of research in higher education, however, no agreed-upon definition of research exists.

Notwithstanding the universal acceptance of the role of research in higher education, however, no agreed-upon definition of research exists. Rather, the word "research" is a general term used in a variety of ways by the different constituencies in higher education. These various groups each use the term in a way that reflects their particular philosophical and political perspectives. In particular, a number of differences in use across disciplines are of considerable significance but are not as yet entirely understood. Such differences need to be appreciated by all with a vested interest in higher education: faculty, administrators, policy makers, funding bodies, and the wider community. To understand these different uses of the word "research," this section investigates research in its various forms within the setting of higher education and the nature and extent of its connection with the role of teaching.

General Characteristics of University Research

One way of beginning to grapple with the topic is to look at those attributes of university research applicable to all fields and disciplines. A number of well-established features distinguish university research:

1. Research receives its main impetus from problems defined

*within the framework of a discipline. That is, the contri-
bution that a research project may make to the field is the
primary consideration, with any direct economic or social
benefits being secondary. As a result, both research proposals and outcomes are judged mainly on the basis of
excellence rather than [on] their immediate utility in
terms of direct industrial or social relevance.*

2. *Both individual researchers and their departments/centres
require a high level of freedom from external interfer-
ence. . .to adequately pursue specific research goals
[and] the general purposes of higher education.*

3. *An integral part of the research process is the publishing
of results for scrutiny by other researchers.*

4. *Diversity in approach is valued and fostered. Consequently, research is conducted in many different
ways. . . .*

5. *The majority of academics are involved in both teaching
and research, although* [the balance varies, depending on
preference, capability, and stage of career] (Neumann and
Lindsay 1988, pp. 308–9).

Although these characteristics apply to research in all disciplines within a university, research is not a homogeneous phe-
nomenon. This list of characteristics describes the orientation of
university research, but to proceed further, we must explore
what is understood by the term ''research'' as used by the different disciplines.

The Notion of Research: Its Scope and Orientation
The term ''research'' is not easily defined. It covers a wide
range of activities, some of which have evolved over a long
period of time. Research studies, both quantitative (Biglan
1973a, 1973b) and qualitative (Becher 1981, 1987a, 1987b;
McGrath 1962), have demonstrated that different fields have
different understandings of the term, how it should be conducted, and what its relationship to other areas of academic
work, teaching in particular, should be. Such studies suggest
that an understanding of ''research'' is best gained by looking
at the context within which the term is used. Each discipline
has its own knowledge paradigm, which determines the appropriate manner of approaching a research problem. Hence, in
some disciplines ''research'' is what is done in ''projects,''
whereas in others it involves field work or laboratory experi-

mentation and in others still is the study of documents in a library. The diverse activities carried out by different fields under the umbrella of research include scholarship, construction of theories, observing and chronicling, experimentation, testing theories, design, development, criticizing and elucidating, artistic creation, and consulting and advising (Carter 1980). According to some viewpoints, not all of these activities are legitimately described as "research"; they may be labeled instead as "community service" or grouped along with "scholarship" as a category distinct from "research." In general terms, two types of views are prevalent about what constitutes research. The broad view takes into account disciplinary differences and highlights the wide and diverse range of research activities in different settings; the narrower view includes only the discovery of new knowledge, often with an emphasis on quantitative techniques.

Support for a broad view comes from the research on academic disciplines and culture. A landmark study (Biglan 1973a, 1973b) identified three dimensions that characterize the subject matter of academic areas: (1) the extent to which a paradigm exists; (2) the weight placed on the application of research findings to practical problems; and (3) concern for "life systems." These different dimensions of the orientation of research play a powerful role in the structure of a discipline and the form of its research output as well as provide a model for understanding and studying the different cognitive styles of academics. The application of this model to the broad range of disciplines found within universities produced empirical evidence that different values, beliefs, and patterns of work exist in the subject areas. Differences were found in preferences for the type of research conducted; the number of sources of influence on research goals; the form of reporting research results; the degree of collaboration in research and teaching; relations with staff and students, especially research students; and emphases on teaching and service.

Another study (Becher 1981, 1987a, 1987b) involved an investigation of academic culture. British and American academics in six discipline groups, covering the humanities, social sciences, sciences, and professional areas, were interviewed to build up an image of the nature of academic disciplines. This approach yielded valuable insights into the similarities and differences of research both within and between the six discipline areas and highlighted how a qualitative approach can be used to illuminate the process of intellectual investigation as well as the values, beliefs, and traditions influencing this process. Becher analyzed the interview data to contrast the disciplines and ascertained that the differences in the practices, beliefs, and values held by the various disciplines were far more noticeable than any epistemological distinctions between them. For example, despite their different epistemological foundations, disciplines like biology and history, with a well-established tradition and long-standing amateur involvement, stressed above all else clarity of expression and avoidance of technical language. Becher found that the use of language within disciplines and their method of collecting and presenting evidence demonstrated the shared values within disciplines and their different epistemological approaches. Each discipline was not homogeneous, however; it was dynamic and creative, reflecting different research emphases and trends at different times and in different countries, while still sharing a strong international culture. Flexibility and diversity in the approach to research were common to all disciplines, however.

These studies demonstrate that the term "research" has multiple interpretations, is multidimensional, and is discipline-dependent. Their findings indicate that the generalizability of the notion of research and the transferability of its meaning from one academic area to another are limited. This finding has crucial implications for the generalizability of notions of excellence and utility in research, for methods of evaluating research proposals and performance, and for research policy and funding generally. Lack of appreciation of the broad scope and diverse orientations to research and the adoption of a narrow definition of "research" by policy makers and funding bodies could lead to a loss of flexibility, diversity, and vitality in the research activity of universities. One of the great strengths of the American research system in comparison to those of European countries has been its diversity and decentralization (Geiger 1985b).

Unfortunately, governments and their agencies commonly ignore these different contextual notions of research as they increasingly adopt a narrow notion of "research" biased primarily toward the physical sciences (OECD 1987). Within the prevailing mode of thought, such a definition provides a convenient rationale for targeting funding on those research areas perceived to have economic or military potential.

Justifications for policies of the concentration of research and the selectivity of research projects, researchers, and institutions also draw on this restricted view of research. Such policies are being increasingly used to favor a select range of disciplines and institutions. The utility and relevance of the humanities, social sciences, and the less prestigious natural sciences are especially vulnerable to being neglected over the longer term (Neumann and Lindsay 1987, 1988; OECD 1987, p. 101).

The narrow notion of what constitutes research is based on the view that a dichotomy exists between "research" and "scholarship." Research involves exploring the new frontiers of knowledge, while scholarship is seen as keeping up to date with the research literature in one's field, especially in fields with few new frontiers of knowledge left. Thus, in this view, real research consists of theorizing, experimenting, and testing theories and applies for all practical purposes only to the "hard" quantitative sciences—particularly to the expensive forms, such as high-energy physics. This dichotomous view is also used to link "research" with "science" and with social or economic value, while "scholarship" is applied to the humanities and implies private benefit to the individual rather than the community (Cyert and Knapp 1984).

The view that research and scholarship are distinct activities is tenable but not fully convincing. If we take the traditional way of defining terms by establishing a class and then identifying distinguishing characteristics of each genus (Copi 1961), it is clear that all the activities listed earlier have, on a general level, the common characteristics of being investigative, systematic, and creative. At a more specific level, however, each activity has some distinguishing features. Not all involve, at least to the same extent, the production of new knowledge. If then the feature of creating new knowledge is taken to be the distinguishing feature of "research," some activities may fall into a different category that can be labeled "scholarship."

Nevertheless, in terms of actual use, scholars do not agree on whether research and scholarship are separate categories of activity. Some commentators maintain that a dichotomy exists (see, for example, Carter 1980). Others argue that "scholarship" involves more than simply keeping abreast with the research literature in a field, as it also includes interpreting anew existing knowledge (see, for example, Elton 1986; Schwartzman 1984). In this view, scholarship is a necessary component of the research process in all fields, because it is a vital component of the procedure of theory construction. As such, "scholarship" is also "research."

From this viewpoint, the contention that scholarship belongs to the realm of the humanities and research to the sciences would be rejected on the grounds that the reevaluation and reinterpretation of past thought are inextricably linked with the development of new theories, which is a central activity in all disciplines. An argument against the dichotomous view maintains that:

> Like their colleagues in accepted scientific disciplines, researchers in the humanities try to develop theories, to analyze data, to build models and test them, with the objective of explaining the issues they study (Cyert and Knapp 1984, p. 96).

Further weight is added to this argument by the claim that the German word *Wissenschaft* has a much broader meaning than the English translation "science." It incorporates the English notion of "scholarship" as well as being the German word for "knowledge" (Elton 1986; Flexner 1979, pp. 102–3; Schwartzman 1984). In fact, the understanding of the German *Wissenschaft* is crucial. It refers to any organized body of knowledge and is used as a suffix to name disciplines. The broad groupings of knowledge are described as *Geisteswissenschaften* (humanities), *Naturwissenschaften* (natural sciences), and *Sozialwissenschaften* (social sciences). To describe a piece of work as *wissenschaftlich* is to talk of its sound scholarship or to describe it as being well researched. Indeed, some work relates the word *Wissenschaft* with the Greek *philosophia*, both words incorporating far more than the English word "science," which, although it has its origin in the Latin word for "knowledge" (*scientia*), now implies certain methodological approaches (Ringer 1969, pp. 102–4).

It also must be remembered that historically our view of the status of knowledge has influenced our notion of research and that as the weight we give to certain types of knowledge changes, so does the interpretation of what constitutes "research." Research in universities has developed from the medieval view of research (some would say "scholarship") as elucidating or glossing the authoritative texts to master what was considered to be the universal and absolute knowledge.

Later, this belief that knowledge was absolute gave way to the notion that knowledge was tentative and could be revised, overthrown, or extended. Hence, the still-current belief developed that one of the functions of a university was to advance knowledge.

Nevertheless, the "new" knowledge of the 19th century university was built on the firmly established medieval tradition, moving from the refining of knowledge to the discovery of new facts. The development of critical analysis and seminar research techniques in the humanities in the late 18th and early 19th centuries laid the foundation stones of *Wissenschaftsideologie*—the view of knowledge as dynamic and creative (Turner 1971). Independent research and critical, analytic methods applicable to specialized areas of knowledge were pioneered in the areas of philology, philosophy, and history and became the standard for all other disciplines. To be accepted into the universities and be able to compete with the humanities, the sciences, which had in the 17th century developed outside the universities and in accord with practical applications of the knowledge, also began to cultivate pure research, specialization, and publication.

Flexner's examination of the development of knowledge and its relations to research and the curriculum in American higher education (1979) explains how, in the latter half of the 19th century, Americans returned from study in Germany using the term "scientific research." This term was derived by combining two words originating from two different contexts within the German idea of a university. The result was to place on the term a narrow methodological interpretation of "specifically scientific." During the 20th century, particularly the latter half, this narrow interpretation has become the increasingly dominant interpretation in Western universities. The narrowing of the term "research" has been accelerated by the stringent financial situation in universities, the increasing cost of scientific equipment, and the concern by governments for immediate economic returns from research. This trend has particular implications for the way the notions of excellence and utility are used in discussing and assessing research, which will be addressed in a later section.

Research and Its Nexus with Teaching

Historically, the function of research in universities has clearly evolved in close relationship with the function of teaching. Although universities originally provided professional training in areas such as law, theology, and medicine, in conjunction with this function of teaching was a major concern with the notion of scholarship, which involved reflection, appraisal, and commentary on existing knowledge. This process contributed to the preservation of knowledge. The late 18th century German *Wissenschaftsideologie*, which emphasized the creativity and dynamism of learning, grew out of this tradition of scholarship and critical argument. In the early 19th century, German scholars, initially in philology, philosophy, and history, began developing seminars oriented toward techniques of research inquiry, providing training for specialists rather than generalists, and enabling students to carry out independent investigations. It was at that time too that the revolutionary new practice of lecturing directly from the material of an academic's research was instigated (Turner 1971, pp. 148–49). Belief in the close connection between teaching and research became embodied in the Humboldtian idea of the unity of teaching and research, which became one of the cardinal principles of German, American, and British universities and has continued into the 20th century (Redner 1987).

This historical development of the function of research alongside the function of teaching has convinced many scholars that a teaching-research nexus exists that is vital and indispensable to academic work. The interconnection of teaching and research has become a basic organizational feature of universities and is found at all levels, from the institutional to the individual academic. The disciplines provide the organizational framework for universities. The basic unit, whether it be the department, the school, or the center, usually reflects a single discipline or a cluster of related disciplines. The "professional" colleges and departments, while oriented toward the profession concerned, still have a disciplinary focus. Thus, universities are structured to reflect the division of knowledge. The search for new knowledge largely takes place through these disciplinary structures that have evolved and continue to develop in response to the requirements of research. As new areas of knowledge have emerged through the progress of research, departments have proliferated. The teaching role in universities mirrors the research-based structures, with the overall course patterns, the organization of knowledge into subjects, the approach to each subject, and the inherent attitudes and values of each field all reflecting past and current developments in esearch. Thus, both teaching and research take place within a disciplinary framework that has been shaped by the accumulation of research—which is not to deny that the overall development of universities has been shaped by interaction with society but merely to assert that, in universities, teaching responds most directly to developments in research, which in turn is influenced by social, political, and economic forces.

As a result of these multilayered connections, teaching, especially from the senior undergraduate and honors years on in the British system and in the graduate schools in American research universities, is not only closely informed by research but also gains its essential substance and direction from research. The involvement in teaching by academics active in research is an important means of maintaining contact with the needs of students and consequently the need to be able to communicate clearly about research as well as a way of placing research within the broader spectrum of the content of knowledge in the field. At the graduate level, teaching and research are not merely interrelated but partly merge. The output of a student's research and that of the student's supervisor often come from a joint production process in which the research process and the research training process have common elements. Indeed, through the dissertation, graduate students make an important contribution to university research.

Differing views exist of course on the teaching-research nexus. Some commentators are skeptical about whether it even exists and demand tangible evidence. They ignore the historical development and the organizational structure of universities or doubt their impact. The skeptics claim that most justifications of its existence and importance are based on conventional wisdom rather than on evidence from empirical research, which is indeed sorely lacking. One reason for the lack of investigation into the existence of the teaching-research nexus is that a tendency exists for academics not to like researching themselves (Flood-Page 1973). Other difficulties in establishing such a connection are because of the lack of definition of what is meant by "teaching" and by "research" and oversimplified formulations by researchers of questions relating to the existence and nature of the teaching-research nexus (Elton 1986).

For example, in discussions of the teaching-research nexus, the notion of scholarship is often given the narrower meaning described earlier, which differentiates it from research by restricting it to "having a good knowledge of the field" and "keeping abreast of the literature." This approach results in the identification of links between advanced teaching and scholarship rather than research. Further, as scholarship and research are often regarded as synonymous in the humanities but not in the sciences, some investigators of the teaching-research nexus claim that the nexus is more a feature of the humanities than the natural sciences.

If the broad view of research is adopted in recognition of the disciplinary variations and the notion embodied in the German word *Wissenschaft*, however, then scholarship is also a necessary component of research in the natural sciences, and it follows that the connection between teaching and research ought to be just as strong. Another way of emphasizing the connection is to focus on the learning that is the object of university teaching and argue that learning and research in a university are related, indeed synonymous, and that the teaching-research nexus resides in their common concern with learning.

Studies on faculty work patterns (see, for example, Pelz and Andrews 1966) indicate that the involvement of academics in both teaching and research is a fruitful one in regard to research output. Reviews of studies of the performance of individual faculty, however, show that they have generally only tested the link between simple measures of research productivity and teaching effectiveness as measured by student ratings (Finkelstein 1984; Friedrich and Michalak 1983; Michalak and Friedrich 1981). A meta-analysis of such studies found only small positive, but statistically insignificant, associations between scholarly accomplishment or research productivity and teaching proficiency (Feldman 1987). The analysis also drew the extremely tentative conclusion that such positive connections were more likely to occur and to be stronger in the humanities and social sciences than in the natural sciences. The study usefully draws together much of the existing research on the teaching-research nexus as related to productivity in research and students' perceptions of teaching effectiveness, but, as Feldman points out, the studies reviewed were of variable quality and did not necessarily take into account the number of different methods of determining research productivity and teaching effectiveness, and the literature itself on this topic contains several major gaps in information. Hence, it is not surprising that little correlation between teaching effectiveness and research productivity has been found.

In any event, investigation of the teaching-research nexus

hould be focused not on establishing its existence at the level
•f the individual academic but rather, because of the wide
ange of work patterns across disciplines, on its existence at the
:vel of the department or even the institution. Certainly, the
trength of belief in the teaching-research nexus varies with dis-
:ipline, influenced by what faculty in different subject areas
inderstand by the term as well as their work preferences (Big-
an 1973b).

Moreover, a review of the literature on research productivity
iotes that most of the studies examining the teaching-research
iexus have focused on the influence of research on teaching,
iot the stimulation and support that teaching gives to research
Dill 1986, p. 10). Even in teaching introductory courses, fac-
ilty may develop questions or lines of inquiry that may not
iave otherwise occurred to them, while graduate students may
nake direct inputs into faculty research.

Thus, belief in the importance of the nexus between research
ind teaching is especially strong at the graduate level. For ex-
imple, a panel session at one annual meeting of the Council of
Jraduate Schools concluded that:

> . . .research and graduate education in the United States are
> inseparable and should be inseparable and that we have a
> fabulously successful system, the premier system in the
> world, of developing research scientists and scholars (White
> 1982, p. 13).

The view was advanced that while primary and secondary education lags in international comparisons and undergraduate standards are about even, graduate education excels because of the
inseparable combination of research and graduate education.

Quite possibly, however, the unity of teaching and research
has been achieved only in a few periods in history and then
only in a few elite institutions, such as the University of Berlin
in the 19th century and in American graduate schools (Ben-
David 1977; Schwartzman 1984; Standing Conference 1964).
After the early decades of the research ethic, an ever-widening
gulf grew between what was practically useful to professional
groups and the degree of specialization required in a particular
field (Ben-David 1977). In addition, many fields arose as a result of research that were unconnected to any area of professional practice. Only in America did the graduate schools cater
to the professions that required a high level of sophistication

and specialization and provide the training for the next generation of researchers to perpetuate and advance the discipline.

Others believe that the teaching-research nexus is weakening as traditional university values are replaced with those of the "multiversity" (Redner 1987, p. 54). The "multiversity" with its embrace of all areas of study—technical, practical, the old and the new professions, the arts and culture—has led to a negation of the principle of the unity of teaching and research. One reason for it is that some areas of study are of a higher status and consequently are allowed to become distanced from undergraduate teaching. The higher status and rewards of research in general also encourage a retreat from undergraduate teaching, and it has been argued that the multiversity, compared with the traditional, "monistic" university, was based more on conflict and interaction than on unity and integration (Kerr 1972, p. 140). Associated with these multiple goals and consequent uncertainty about direction is external pressure from governments to increase research productivity in certain fields through a separation of teaching and research. Governments increasingly consider the close interconnection of teaching and research to be merely a shibboleth or an inefficient relic of the past (Carter 1980; Dawkins 1987; OECD 1987; Williams and Blackstone 1983).

It can also be argued that competition for a faculty member's time and effort results in a conflict rather than a nexus between the two functions. In teaching, faculty expend effort on knowledge that can no longer be investigated, compared with the effort in research expended on knowledge that cannot be taught yet because it still needs investigating. Teaching and research thus have different aims and need different approaches, talents, and facilities (Ben-David 1977, pp. 93–94). An examination of the argument that more time spent on research conflicts with faculty's teaching responsibilities concluded, however, that the available evidence did not support this argument at all (Feldman 1987).

The modern specialization and departmentalization of knowledge also cause a tension between the breadth of undergraduate teaching and the specialized research interests of the faculty. The conflict is also seen in the difference between a good research library with its single copy of recent relevant material and a good undergraduate teaching library with a much smaller range of more introductory materials, some in multiple copies.

A similar situation exists in laboratory equipment and computing facilities (Williams 1984).

The harmony and the conflict between teaching and research arise from the existence within institutions of higher education of two different sets of values—the collegiate and the disciplinary (Clark 1983). The collegiate values of teaching and the institution stand juxtaposed to those of research and the discipline. Because of their involvement in both teaching and research, faculty operate in both camps and are hence governed by both sets of values. Thus, a history department, for example, operates both in the institution within which it resides and the discipline itself, which in concrete terms is the sum of all history departments. As a result, the faculty members in this history department operate on two levels. For research, they relate to the discipline and are thereby in contact with other faculty with similar research interests within the discipline of history in other universities, nationally and internationally. Teaching, however, while being the means of transmitting the knowledge of the discipline, takes place within the institutional setting and brings faculty members into contact with faculty with completely different research interests and in different disciplines within the university.

Over time, the values of the discipline have become the dominant values. The disciplinary values, for example, have become the norms on which the appointment and promotion of faculty are based. What counts is active involvement in research, evidenced in the publication of research results for scrutiny by other researchers in the field. These values have become so dominant that those institutions with little or no previous involvement in research are moving toward research roles for their faculty. The rationale for this trend includes improving institutional quality and the important and intimate connection between teaching and research (Bassis and Guskin 1986; Haneman 1975). Further evidence of the dominance of research over teaching comes from a recent qualitative study of three faculty generations at a large research-oriented land-grant university that investigated the professional socialization and career attitudes of faculty (Corcoran and Clark 1984). Each successive cohort showed an increase in the socialization into the values of a research university, and this process was most pronounced in the latest (1970) cohort. From the early stages, faculty demonstrated a marked preference for research over teaching, although dominant interest in research did not necessarily convey a lack of interest in teaching or working with students.

Summary

Research in higher education is characterized by diverse orientations and approaches. Its main impetus comes from problems defined in a disciplinary context, and the disciplinary culture of a shared endeavor and peer review provides the framework. The disciplines differ quite markedly in their notion of research, particularly in its integration with or separation from "scholarship." The current trends in policy tend to favor a restricted notion of research and those sciences with immediate utility to economic or military goals.

Three sets of views apply to the teaching-research nexus: One group believes in its existence and importance, another questions its existence, calling for more direct evidence, and a third claims that this nexus has developed into one of conflict, so that a teaching-research conflict exists in place of the teaching-research nexus. Appropriate conclusions are not easily reached on this complex and contentious topic:

The relationship between research and teaching is such a myth-laden subject that precise and broadly accepted generalization is almost impossible to make (Mayhew 1973, p. 29).

Four general conclusions seem to be justified, however:

1. Teaching and research have historically developed in close relationship;
2. Belief in the importance of the teaching-research nexus is generally strong among faculty, especially as it relates to the graduate level;
3. In practice both connections and conflicts exist between teaching and research; and
4. Internal developments in some disciplines, particularly the expensive sciences, and external pressures tend to weaken the connections.

EXCELLENCE AND UTILITY IN HARMONY AND CONFLICT

The Relationship between Excellence and Utility

Through the centuries, notions of excellence and utility have played an important part in shaping the form and culture of higher education. The medieval universities adapted the classical notion of excellence to fit intellectual virtuosity, achieved by exercising innate abilities through rigorous logic. In the 19th century, excellence became linked to the advancement of knowledge for its own sake. At various times, utility has resided in mastery of the prevailing mode of thought, at others in questioning its foundations. Thus, over time both excellence and utility have changed their meaning. Their relationship to each other has also varied from harmonious coexistence to direct conflict. Of the many forms and variations of the relationship between excellence and utility in higher education, four are especially important:

At issue is whether the excellence of the elite can coexist with the mediocrity of mass higher education.

Excellence emphasized at the expense of utility

In this version, excellence is the praiseworthy pursuit of knowledge for its own sake in the best traditions of the epistemological philosophy, while utility is an irrelevant or competing concern tainted by overtones of commercialism, the second rate, and the inferiority of the applied in comparison to the prestige of the pure and the abstract. The focus of research is on contributing to the discipline, and the problems, methods, and values operating reflect the advancement of knowledge as a self-justifying activity. Teaching also is directed toward enabling students to master the discipline with the ultimate aim of being able to undertake research. Both the classical and the Humboldtian traditions reflect this viewpoint. Its strength is reflected in and fostered by the academic reward system. This system is one that recognizes values and hence rewards certain types of research. It is discipline oriented, rewarding those academics with promotion and peer recognition who contribute to the progress of knowledge within the discipline. As a result, basic research is valued above applied, excellence above utility.

Utility emphasized at the expense of excellence

In this version, excellence in fostering knowledge for its own sake is a code word for faculty self-indulgence and the neglect of human considerations and society's problems, while utility, standing for relevance to human needs, is the worthwhile goal. Research is directed toward problems of practical significance that by their nature often require a multidisciplinary approach.

In teaching, the concern is to develop competencies useful to students in their careers and later life. The justification for higher education in this viewpoint is political rather than epistemological, and the institutional role is clearly oriented toward service.

Utility in teaching and excellence in research
This variation combines elements of the first two versions by linking teaching to utility and research to excellence. Teaching can be seen as the expression of utility for several reasons. From the point of view of the student and of society, teaching is useful for the preparation of students for the various professions. Indeed, this preparation has been a function of universities since the Middle Ages, and the number and type of professional groups accommodated have gradually broadened from the traditional areas of theology, medicine, and law to include engineering, architecture, computer science, and a host of other professional and technological areas. Utility resides not only in the usefulness of the particular knowledge learned but also in the completion of a course of study that qualifies the student for a certain type of career. The range of professional preparation also includes the training of the next generation of researchers, which maintains the academic profession and its useful teaching function as well as the national research establishment that, with the intimate connection between science and the economy in modern industrial societies, is of crucial value to the society (Schwartzman 1984, p. 206; Turner 1971). And finally, teaching represents utility because it is through professional preparation that academics transmit the core knowledge of a discipline to students. Teaching thus serves the end of the discipline itself, providing for its continuity. Research on the other hand is directed toward the pursuit of excellence as in the first version, because it is through the advancement of knowledge within a discipline, based on the problems inherent within the discipline, that the frontiers of knowledge are extended.

Excellence in utility
This variation is the distinctively American contribution to higher education's role—excellence in the service of the nation. In this version, excellence is just as important in problem solving as in the advancement of abstract fields. The goal is to be excellent in pursuing some human need, whether solving a social or economic problem or undertaking that fundamental hu-

man need: research driven by curiosity. This viewpoint tries to harmonize the influences of the epistemological and political justifications in a diverse pluralistic approach that tries to accommodate possibly conflicting goals.

In practice, of course, these viewpoints are not so clear cut, and they operate simultaneously within the rather chaotic culture of higher education. They represent different answers to the question of whether harmony can exist between community service and the traditional functions of teaching and research— between the American land-grant model in which the university is conceived as an instrument of economic and social progress and the German and British models with their emphasis on a strong commitment to the value of free and independent inquiry, to the love of knowledge for its own sake, and to the importance of mental discipline. At issue is whether the excellence of the elite can coexist with the mediocrity of mass higher education and whether a commitment to the philosophy of community service compromises and ultimately erodes a commitment to the traditional functions of teaching and research (Ross 1967, p. 10).

The Question of Standards

One basic concern underlying these relationships between excellence and utility is the issue of standards. Set within the context of educational evaluation, the notion of excellence involves performing at an appropriate standard. To give content to the notion, standards must be set and evaluation procedures developed. In theory, standards of excellence may be either norm-referenced or criterion-referenced. If the standard is norm-referenced, a performance to be excellent must surpass that of the other participants. If the evaluation is criterion-referenced, the standard is defined independently of the distribution of performance. In practice, however, whether couched in relative or absolute terms, the setting of standards is not an arbitrary choice. To be functional in the social, economic, and political setting, the standards of excellence must be defined so that only the very few will achieve it. Excellence defined in other ways would lose its utility. Where excellence relates to some ability that is a commodity exchangeable for other benefits, excellence is a quite utilitarian notion carrying a monetary value. In science, for example, it has been claimed that the best is much more important than the second best (Ford Foundation 1977), and the economic importance of international scientific leadership increasingly demonstrates the cogency of this claim.

This emphasis on high standards causes unease in those concerned with equality. Within the educational literature, the elitist connotations of excellence and its compatibility with a concern for equity have been major issues (see, for example, Gardner 1961; Strike 1985). Two strategies are advocated to counter the elitism of excellence. The first is to emphasize a pluralistic approach in which many different kinds of excellence and a variety of criteria are recognized. Within this diversity, the second strategy is to assess excellence in terms of one's own previous performances rather than in comparison with others. Nevertheless, higher education is "basically a sorting mechanism on the basis of excellence" (Premfors 1982, p. 374), and so trade-offs between excellence and equality must occur. Indeed, in all Western countries, the view has been growing that the trade-offs have gone too far toward favoring equality over excellence.

Excellence in What?

Also at issue in these viewpoints on excellence and utility is the extent to which a particular answer to the question "Excellence in what?" harmonizes or reduces the conflict between them. Excellence is not only a powerful word but one "that means different things to different people" (Gardner 1961, p. xii). It is not just a question of differing judgments but different varieties of excellence. Excellence in art, management, and parenting, for example, involves quite different kinds of excellence. In the intellectual domain alone, many kinds of excellence exist. Some kinds of excellence can be fostered by the education system, others outside. Some kinds of excellence are valued and rewarded by society; others may not be.

In essence, then, it is the nature of the activity in which excellence is being pursued that is of central concern. References to "excellence" and to the "pursuit of excellence" are common in the literature on higher education, particularly in discussions of goals and functions. Such references are often ritualistic rather than expressive and substantive statements. Neither the notion nor its referent activity is clearly defined. In general terms, however, both teaching and research can be conceived as being largely directed toward achieving intellectual excellence. Excellence is thus linked to knowledge, the fundamental commodity in higher education. Knowledge has been developed and organized into disciplines or fields over many years, even centuries, in a process that reflects both universities' independence from and connection to their wider society. Within the range of different orientations to knowledge that have existed over time and across the disciplines, the level of utility perceived at any one time has varied considerably. Thus, excellence in both teaching and research is sought in activities with varying types and degrees of utility.

A further source of variation is the decentralization of responsibility for determining and maintaining academic quality and excellence. Standards are determined by the judgments of individual faculty and departments. Because of the fragmentation of knowledge and the widespread adherence to the mystical view of quality, peer review within the disciplines is the cornerstone of judgment. This disciplinary and departmental determination of standards leads to substantial variations within institutions and, even more so, across institutions (Folger 1984).

The Narrowing of Excellence and Utility

Changes in Western societies and their higher education systems over the last 30 years have led to a narrowing in meaning for both excellence and utility. This narrowing has heightened the conflict between them and lessened the potential for harmony. Throughout its history, the development of higher education has been justified on utilitarian grounds. The expansion of higher education in Western countries after World War II was no exception, premised as it was on the economic and social benefits of scientific research and a more educated work force. In the United States, Vannevar Bush, science adviser to President Roosevelt, portrayed science as an "endless frontier." Guided by this vision, the federal government became a generous patron of basic science in the belief that it would make an essential and decisive contribution to the improvement of society. The partnership between government and university research was predicated on the assumption that the cultivation of excellence was the way to obtain the most productive results from the investment in science (Ford Foundation 1977).

The postwar expansion, it can be argued, was a straight extrapolation of trends established in the late 19th century that allowed universities to fulfill their proper destinies, only with American institutions replacing the German universities as the pacesetters for the world. An alternative view is that the actions

of governments have distorted the nature of higher education to the detriment of its total mission (Standing Conference 1964). Certainly, the national preoccupation with research and its rewards has tempted many institutions to seek excellence in research and graduate education for which they have neither the traditions nor the resources (Mayhew 1973, p. 18).

The scale and form of the postwar expansion was such that higher education was firmly established as a pivotal institution in society. With this irreversible change to higher education's role, its utility became a major preoccupation of governments. Both the growth in research and the growth in numbers of students were justified in terms of potential economic benefits. The skeptics expressed concern about the changing nature of higher education, but their voices "were drowned out by the jingling of hard cash" (Phillips 1982, p. 7). The scale of the expansion and the consequent importance that higher education assumed for society, however, irreversibly changed higher education's function and the basis of its legitimacy. The economic rationale underlying the expansion resulted in changes to subjects' hierarchy of status. Subjects were classified as either "useful" or "useless (though desirable)" on the basis of whether they had clear and immediate utility (Blume 1982, p. 13). The natural sciences, regarded as useful or potentially so, received relatively generous funding, while the social sciences strove to emulate their more affluent neighbors and hence gain access to the largesse of research funding. The humanities were designated as useless and therefore subject to neglect. Indeed, it can be argued, the humanities themselves contributed to these trends by failing to criticize their utilitarian nature and by not demonstrating to themselves, other disciplines, and society that they had important contributions to make (Bloom 1987).

Thus, while higher education policy was directed at a fairly general expansion of student numbers, research policy was essentially "science" policy and was directed at the expansion of scientific research. In keeping with the faith in the benefits of science and the prosperity of the times, the expansion encompassed both basic and applied science.

The higher education systems that were undergoing this utilitarian expansion, however, were the heirs of von Humboldt's model of a university in which the epistemological justification overshadowed the political one. Indeed, although governments premised the postwar expansion on utility, much of the effect within the universities was to reinforce the epistemological philosophy. The massive injection of funds into basic research resulted in rapid advances in knowledge—and consequently narrower specialization—in many disciplines, especially the natural sciences. Theory became increasingly abstract and removed from everyday events and problems, fostering a rather inward-looking stance in many disciplines. This focus on basic research has led to the neglect of attempts to solve the practical problems of society. Indeed, private organizations like the think tanks in Washington, Boston, and the Silicon Valley have now taken over part of the applied research once undertaken by higher education institutions (Schuh 1986).

As a consequence of these trends, excellence came to be increasingly judged and, in extreme cases, solely judged in terms of a contribution to the discipline's framework of knowledge. Thus, the modern research university has become introverted into an orientation to disciplinary peers rather than an orientation to its constituents in society, leading to increasingly narrow and single-criterion concepts of academic excellence. This increasing abstraction and specialization have also led to increasing irrelevance (Lynton and Elman 1987; Schuh 1986). A comparative study of faculty views of the nature of scholarship in research universities and selective liberal arts colleges found that faculty in the latter were critical of the work of their disciplines:

> They perceive their fields to be preoccupied with narrow, specialized topics and marginal, incremental contributions to an arcane literature (Ruscio 1987, p. 213).

The humanities and social sciences have been particularly inward-looking and ill-disposed toward recognizing the value of other, even related, disciplines (Bloom 1987).

In the context of the postwar economic boom, Western societies and their governments acquiesced to the accompanying accumulation of power by the academic and research communities. Over the last 15 years, however, economic decline and increased international competition in manufacturing have led to a renewed emphasis on the utility of research (Cragg 1984; Press 1982). Indeed, throughout the Western world the trend for some time has been toward narrowing the notion of utility to mean having immediate technological applications bringing economic benefits.

Simultaneously, governments have sought to achieve tighter

control over university research. In many countries, a more long-term and comprehensive national policy for research is being developed in response to the heavy economic inputs now required for advanced research and the national economic importance of such research (Geiger 1985b; Wittrock 1985b). This trend is affecting government research institutions as well as the universities. First government researchers in engineering laboratories and then biomedical researchers in the National Institutes of Health have been compelled by the Technology Transfer Act of 1986 to grapple with the opportunities and problems of close collaboration with industry (Booth 1989).

Thus, the narrow notion of excellence associated with the epistemological justification and a concentration of power in academia clashes head on with the notion of utility expounded by governments seeking to redirect universities toward their economic goals. Although fueled by the funding boom, the pecking order of disciplines has become even more differentiated with the advent of austerity by the inherent biases of the current trends in policy. The leveling off in federal support for university research in the late 1960s was accompanied by greater emphasis on targeted research with its short-term goals. The growth in contract research concentrated funding on those fields perceived to be able to solve current problems or meet national needs.

Much of the renewed growth in funding for university research has been for military or commercial purposes, which has led to considerable debate about the impact of requirements for secrecy on university research. Many universities have developed policies on conflict of interest and allowed some form of delay in publication (Burke 1985). Nevertheless, if publication of results is delayed or prohibited, the potential contribution of the research to the development of knowledge is inhibited as is the process of scrutiny by peers, regarded as basic to the maintenance of standards, self-correcting advances, and the pursuit of excellence.

It is apparent that the importance attached to close relationships between universities and their communities has varied over time. Following the establishment and rise to influence of the land-grant universities, the mission of American universities became to address the problems of society and to apply the tools of science and technology to the solution of those problems—hence the familiar tripartite mission of teaching, research, and service. In the 1970s, collaboration between universities and industry was considered dubious and preferably to be avoided for the sake of universities' liberty and independence. This attitude has gradually been revised in the aftermath of the oil crisis and the resultant economic decline. Cooperation and close relations have come to be invested with positive value. Indeed, the demands for immediately useful and applicable research findings have become so insistent that some researchers are concerned about the long-term future. This trend has been most marked in the technologies, in scientific and medical research, and in some areas of the social sciences, while the humanities have been hardly affected at all. This trend is a direct result of the interest in productive usefulness, the result of the short-term perspective characteristic of a period of economic decline (Schuh 1986, p. 17).

EXCELLENCE AND UTILITY IN FUNDING RESEARCH

Conflict in the Process of Funding Research

The prevailing notions of excellence and utility come into direct conflict in the process of funding research. At the macro level, overall research budgets are determined by a governmental/bureaucratic decision-making process focused on utility, while at the micro level, project funding is determined through peer review focused on excellence. Thus, at the national level, the decision making relates to extrinsic considerations—the needs and desires of society—while at the institutional level, the intrinsic quality of research proposals is assessed by peer judgments about their excellence in terms of their potential contribution to the discipline or to our understanding of the field (Sams 1975). The two processes are inconsistent and often incompatible, as the decisions about society's needs for research in overall terms and for each broad field and type are made by the political process in the context of overall priorities. These criteria and priorities are then set aside at the micro level by an allocation process of peer review focused on a relatively narrow notion of excellence.

All of which is not to deny that peer review is fundamental to the social organization of disciplines as collective enterprises. The scrutiny of one's research by peers orients the researcher toward contributing to a shared quest. The peer-review system also assists in shielding researchers from social and political pressures that can destroy the independence of mind and detachment necessary for good research. In short, the process reflects the norms of science as expounded by Merton (1973): universalism, communality, disinterestedness, and organized skepticism. Both the advancement of knowledge and the reward system in academia depend upon findings published for scrutiny by others in the field (Gaston 1978). Because peer judgments confer recognition and establish the reputation of a researcher, it is a logical step to use the same type of judgments in the assessment of research proposals.

Funding decisions should be based on broader considerations than usually encompassed by peer review, however, especially when an inward-looking disciplinary stance recognizes excellence only in contributions to the discipline. An exploration of the use of excellence in funding decisions based on peer review and the resulting inconsistency with broader political decisions identifies three underlying assumptions:

At the macro level, overall research budgets are determined by a governmental/bureaucratic decision-making process focused on utility, while at the micro level, project funding is determined through peer review focused on excellence.

1. In most disciplines, sound judgments about excellence can be made only through peer review.
2. Every effort should be made to fund excellent research.
3. Basic science is a largely separable part of the total system of humanity, excellent research consequently should not involve itself in politics, and its only ethical obligation is to report findings honestly (Churchman 1982, p. 109).

Agreement among peers on what constitutes excellence in a particular situation is by no means straightforward. To simplify the process to manageable proportions, those making the judgments tend to arbitrarily narrow the range of considerations and meanings so that "definitions of excellence tend to be most narrow at the point where we are selecting individuals, or testing them, or training them" (Gardner 1961, p. 128). Even so, the level of agreement about excellence in particular cases may not be high. A study of proposals to the NSF found that receiving a grant depends to a significant degree on chance (Cole, Cole, and Simon 1981). The particular choice of reviewers from the pool of eligible experts was identified as an important factor in success.

It is the axiom of separability that is the basic belief, however, and it arises because some aspects of research can be judged by the peer group in isolation from the rest of society (Churchman 1982). Whether or not society should support that research depends not only on the excellence of the procedures and outcomes in contributing to the discipline but also on the value, or potential value, of the outcomes within the priorities of the whole social system. Thus, in deciding whether to support a proposal, ethical and political considerations may be explicit or implicit, but they cannot be avoided.

The determination of research goals and priorities by the governmental/bureaucratic process is also not without problems. Governments tend to adopt short-term perspectives, narrow definitions of utility, and easy solutions to complex problems. They also tend to consider that their own goals are synonymous with national goals (Brickman 1985; Elzinga 1985; Lindsay and Neumann 1987). It must be emphasized, however, that universities have complex and multidimensional relationships with their communities and that their contributions to society are social and cultural as well as economic, long term as well as short term.

In the 1980s, the relationships between higher education and the private sector have become increasingly problematic throughout Western countries, even in those with a previously satisfactory record (OECD 1987). Nevertheless, instead of struggling with the complexities of the relationship, some governments have tended to follow the easier path of adopting general policies encouraging more applied research and development in universities at the expense of basic research. The effect is to focus much university research on present or even past problems rather than on those emerging as crucial for the future. Further, as the outcomes of research, especially basic research, are inherently unknowable and the sources of solutions for practical problems cannot always be foreseen, estimates of the return from investment in research do not provide a sufficient basis for selecting projects. The intangible, diffuse, and long-term nature of research outcomes, particularly in the social sciences and humanities, means that the value of research is often seriously underestimated. Furthermore, despite the efforts of governments, no agreed set of national needs exists at any one time. The different sectors of society have quite different conceptions of what the needs are.

The term "national needs" is often used as a vague unitary notion, but clear categories can be identified: goals allied to national prestige, goals for modernizing the economy, goals for stabilizing economic development, hedonistic goals oriented toward consumers, and goals concerned with scientific development in its own right (Tamas 1980). Similarly, universities have been exhorted to construct an enterprise responsive to national needs in terms of "human well-being, national security, economic stability, and international commercial competitiveness" (Prager 1984, p. 1057).

Too strong an emphasis on mission-oriented research can be seen as a hindrance to the future development of a discipline. The university offered modern science a great advantage during its period of institutionalization of science during the 19th century (Redner 1987, p. 49; Turner 1971). The university protected science in this period from an orientation toward utilitarian goals and from the requirement to provide practical results. This protection proved an advantage in establishing an authoritative body of knowledge, which in the early 19th century the sciences did not have, but which the humanities at that time could lay claim to.

In meeting national needs, the utility of research led by curiosity fostered on the basis of excellence has arguably been as great as that of targeted research. One of the crucial needs at present is:

> . . .*to eliminate misunderstandings concerning the deficient social usefulness of basic research. It has an intrinsic cultural value, it is a necessary precondition of our ability to take part in and benefit from international research, and it constitutes one of the foundation stones of the future development of our country* (Wikstron 1982, p. 15).

Funding Research: National Priorities or Peer Review

It was the decline in levels of research funding that brought out the basic contradiction in the processes of funding research. The contradiction, dormant during the period of prosperity and growth but now at the heart of the matter, is that governments and other funding bodies determine overall budgets for research according to their judgment of the research field's relative utility among the competing claims, but the specific allocation to individual projects is often based on peer reviews that focus on excellence. Typically, between three and five referees evaluate such factors as the "scientific merit" of the proposed research and the ability of the principal investigator. A study of NSF grants found a high correlation between reviewers' ratings of excellence and decisions to award grants but assessments of ability as judged by previous performance apparently not an influential factor (Cole, Cole, and Simon 1981). Proposals from eminent researchers and those from major institutions did not have substantially higher probabilities of success.

The use of the system of peer review to judge excellence as the mechanism for funding research may be regarded as an astute piece of politics on the part of the leaders of the scientific community (Churchman 1982). Clearly, it concentrates power and indeed is one of the cornerstones of academic power. In one sense, peer review represents the establishment, and while its conservative character may embody scholarly skepticism, it may also embody preconceived notions and aversion to risk taking inimical to new developments in a field.

Fields that have a strong paradigm are advantaged in peer review. Where a strong paradigm exists, greater consensus also exists about the priority of research problems to investigate. A high level of agreement among researchers about priorities and approaches to problems makes it easier to compete for research funds, which favors the hard disciplines because the soft areas exhibit more conflict about which direction research should take. It is thus easier for hard areas to demonstrate usefulness in social or economic terms while still maintaining internal standards of excellence.

In keeping with the ethos of peer review, scientific and technical advisory councils tend to be limited in membership to appropriate professionals whose homogeneity and generally well-defined view of their role lead to relatively successful decision making. On the other hand, their impact may be reduced by higher-level political considerations and claims that they are acting against the public interest (Gaziel 1980). Nevertheless, belief in peer review is so strong that the indication of support by the House Science and Technology Committee for broadening the decision-making input to research decisions so that political considerations were placed alongside traditional peer review engendered dismay among researchers at "this politicizing of science" (Lepkowski 1984, p. 19). In part, the faith in peer review can be seen as an example of the mystical view of quality and excellence in operation—the belief that only the initiates in a field can appropriately judge the complex and intangible factors involved.

Despite its fundamental role in maintaining standards and in the self-correcting processes of progress in research, however, the use, especially exclusive use, of peer review in decisions on funding research is not a straightforward issue. It is dysfunctional for the decisions on society's needs for research in overall terms, and for each broad field and type, to be decided within the overall set of societal priorities by the political process and then to have those criteria and priorities set aside by peer review focused on an isolationist notion of excellence. Commitment to a discipline, while a cornerstone of the progress of academic research, has led to excellence's becoming divorced from human purposes and being regarded as an intrinsic good separate from any other considerations.

An overemphasis on pure research into discipline-defined problems at the expense of solving the problems of society through multidisciplinary approaches is at the heart of the separation of, and conflict between, excellence and utility. A way must be found to broaden and link the notions of excellence and utility. To do so, the distinction between basic and applied research should be abolished (Churchman 1982). All research should be "basic" in that it should try to discover reality and "applied" in trying to respond to the most practical problem of all: how to design our lives. In this view, all research should be aimed at a better understanding of the human situation. Consequently, decisions about funding should reflect this basic value.

This view about the ultimate purpose of all research also raises the question of whether decisions should be placed solely in the hands of fellow researchers, for they have no monopoly or even preeminent qualifications for judging the excellence in terms that encompass human needs. Review by peers, narrowly defined as fellow researchers working on the same general problem, may result in the use of narrow self-indulgent notions of excellence with little consideration given to industrial or social relevance or to the broader ethical and political issues. A basic question is thus who should be involved in assessing applications for research grants.

Evaluating Research

For all researchers, evaluation is an indispensable element of the daily experience of research: "Evaluation and community are necessary and natural conditions of growth in science and scholarship" (Sams 1975, p. 19). Thus, a researcher needs to solicit actively the criticism of his or her peers. As the researcher advances in the field, the comfortable supportive relationships with critics in the laboratory or department are replaced by increasingly impersonal, objective, and remote critics. Local and remote judgments can of course differ, and both can be in error in particular cases.

The evaluation of research proposals and programs involves two types of judgment. The first type is the evaluation of the extrinsic, nontechnical factors, such as the research's utility in terms of value to industry, community services, or to state and national interests. A further dimension involves ethical considerations, such as secrecy, restrictions on publication, privacy of personal data, and the health and welfare of subjects. The second type of evaluation relates to strictly scientific or scholarly considerations, such as the potential contribution to knowledge or method, the adequacy of the method and facilities, and the competence of the researcher (Sams 1975).

In theory, the two types of evaluation are distinct, requiring different criteria and qualifications of the assessor, and they are certainly capable of producing mutually contradictory judgments. The tendency is to link the extrinsic considerations to macro-level decision making and the intrinsic to the micro level. Doing so, however, is artificial and contrary to the harmonization of excellence and utility. Both excellence and utility should be considered at all levels, from the national right down to the individual researcher, and all research committees should be constituted accordingly. A broadening of peer review will assist in the assessment of collaborative university/industry research (Brown 1985; Cilley et al. 1986).

As a first step in broadening the process at all levels, the criteria of excellence and utility themselves can be interpreted more broadly. For example, a project's potential contribution can be assessed in terms of:

1. Economics, by the benefits exceeding the costs;
2. Financing, by the level of support attracted;
3. Ethics, by demonstrating the researcher's vitality, integrity, and purpose;
4. Productivity, by making new information of significance available;
5. Professionalism, by clarifying the researcher's status and thereby the hierarchies of intellectual authority;
6. Competition, by evidence of impact through citations, honors, and so on;
7. Methodology, by demonstrating the use, refinement, or development of procedures;
8. Education, by demonstrating the researcher's authority to teach or by contributing to content, research training, recruitment, or institutional status (Sams 1975).

All of these criteria have validity but do not apply with equal force or in all circumstances. Despite the wide disparity in research in terms of the criteria that should apply in its evaluation, however, any research meeting all the appropriate standards may be regarded as meeting the criteria of both excellence and utility.

Excellence has the more general currency as a criterion for funding research across the disciplines than utility, so particular care must be taken not to favor the natural sciences and engineering over the social sciences and humanities by applying a notion of utility biased toward short-term economic benefits. Clearly, the evaluation of research should not be based on a narrow view that differentiates research from scholarship but on a broad view that encompasses the full range of research and scholarly activities performed in the various disciplines.

The second step is to consider the criteria for membership of research committees and review panels. While the primary credential essential for any reviewer is the capacity to judge the excellence of a project in terms of the traditional canons of scholarship, at least some of the reviewers involved should have specific expertise in judging the potential social or economic utility of the research and even its significance for research training and teaching generally.

The more careful selection of reviewers also provides an opportunity to address the growing problem of reviewers with commercial involvement, often undisclosed, in the research topic under review. It is a major problem in the emerging field of biotechnology (Wofsy 1986), and very little is known about "the extent to which faculty are influenced in their research priorities and academic objectivity by their outside professional relationships" (Boyer and Lewis 1985, p. 58). As a safeguard to the integrity of peer review, researchers with substantial commercial interests in a research topic should be excluded from the review process.

This measure will not, however, provide a complete answer to the problem. In some fields, many of the most expert researchers will increasingly have commercial interests. It can also be argued that the universities themselves are being increasingly compromised by university-industry relationships that go "a long way toward committing the university to business values and practices" (Slaughter 1988, p. 254). Devising ways to counter the undesirable aspects of closer links with industry must be given much more attention if multiple university purposes are to be protected.

Other matters not always adequately addressed by the current processes of peer review include academic misconduct and fraud. Universities themselves have a key responsibility to prevent the use of unethical and unsafe research methods and to detect dishonest practices.

Universitywide review committees, providing peer review in the broadest sense, can do much to overcome the inadequacies of narrowly based peer review. Bok (1982) provides a useful discussion of institutional responsibilities and opportunities in this area.

Of greatest concern, however, are the cases where grants are made by external agencies essentially on the basis of potential utility alone. An appropriate recommendation developed by a conference of immunologists is offered:

> *Acceptance by the university of support from any source for a faculty member's research should always be contingent on assurance of adequate provisions for peer review and the absence of conflicts of interest that compromise educational standards and commitment. A standing faculty committee should verify that acceptable standards of review have been met and should, where there is doubt, initiate an appropriate ad hoc review procedure* (Wofsy 1986, p. 486).

PRESSURES ON THE TEACHING ROLE

The changes taking place in the research role will have far-reaching effects on the teaching role of universities, particularly at the doctoral level. Doctoral education stands at the intersection of the policies for higher education, science, and the scientific labor force but has only rarely itself been the subject of explicit policy. Changes often flow from decisions made in the related domains. Both dangers and opportunities can be identified and managed in the current developments in higher education's research role.

The Teaching-Research Nexus

The nexus between teaching and research has been gradually weakening for some time under the influence of both internal and external pressures. Developments within higher education include increasing specialization, a reordering of the disciplines according to perceptions of their utility, and a narrowing in the notion of research. Other internal factors include the supremacy of disciplinary values over collegiate ones and the status and rewards of research. The diversification of higher education's roles, the greater demands on university research for utility and efficiency, and the increasing cost of sophisticated equipment and the consequent concentration of research in major laboratories have also been important influences.

If the nexus between teaching and research is weakened significantly, it will alter the nature and form of students' learning.

If the nexus between teaching and research is weakened significantly, it will alter the nature and form of students' learning. The continual updating of the content taught and a critical orientation toward it are characteristic features of university teaching at all levels, and they are largely sustained by the widespread involvement of faculty in research. An analysis of the demands currently being placed on the research and teaching roles of universities concluded that instead of promoting a separation of the two roles, the teaching-research nexus needs to be reasserted, as only students taught by those informed by current research will be able to manage the pressures of a rapidly changing work environment (OECD 1981). Care must be taken to avoid altering the essential nature of university teaching by isolating it from its basis—open-minded inquiry.

Most important, it is through contact with faculty that students are socialized into the culture of a discipline, which is the first step toward an academic or other research career. Thus, the characteristics of university teaching fostered by the connection with research are particularly crucial for advanced undergraduate and graduate students. With the current trend, undergraduate teaching is in danger of becoming even more divorced from research. Less cross-fertilization of teaching and research, together with less stimulus from faculty actively researching, would be detrimental for undergraduate teaching and could result in fewer undergraduate students' proceeding to graduate study (Neumann and Lindsay 1988). With some of the best students already discouraged by the state of the academic labor market from pursuing advanced graduate education and contemplating an academic career, this situation could develop into a major problem for higher education institutions (Bowen and Schuster 1986, p. 229).

The impact on faculty is also a concern. If the growing separation of teaching and research is unchecked, it will produce separate and distinct classes of teaching-only and research-only faculty. Such a move could have unforeseen and undesirable consequences, leading to rigidities and an unhealthy hierarchy among faculty. At risk are the flexibility in the current system for the mix of research and teaching to vary over a faculty member's career, as well as the benefits to performance in research from involvement in teaching (Creswell 1985; Pelz and Andrews 1966).

Not all the links between teaching and research have proven to be beneficial, however. The increasing need for specialization and concentration of effort in advanced research conflicts with the needs of teaching. Clear benefits accrue in not tying the scale of research in a field to the level of teaching required, although because the faculty numbers in a particular field are largely determined by the number of students, the expansion of research has tended to reflect the expansion of undergraduate education. In recognition of the fact that research needs and priorities may not necessarily parallel those for teaching, the trend in policy has been to separate funding for research from the general provision for teaching. On the other hand, the increase in direct outside funding for research has clearly impaired the ability of presidents and boards to govern their institutions. Thus, no straightforward solutions exist to the dilemmas of the teaching-research nexus in higher education. Traditionally, the size and diversity of higher education in the United States have allowed competing alternatives to exist side by side without the need for trade-offs. With such a fundamental issue as the teaching-research nexus and with the forces at work so powerful and pervasive, such a solution may no longer serve. A pressing need exists for investigation into the costs

nd benefits of the nexus and debate about the desirable pattern
or the future before the decisions are made by default from the
momentum of change in the role of research.

Doctoral Education

n view of the nature and vital importance of doctoral educa-
ion, special consideration should be given to how it may be
affected by changes in research policies and organization. With
ts combination of high-level study and major research project,
the Ph.D. sits at the point where teaching and research in the
university merge. The doctoral student learns the necessary
skills through an apprenticeship and in undertaking research for
the dissertation is also expected to contribute directly to the development of the relevant field. A tension exists between the
"training" and "contribution to knowledge" of the Ph.D., and
the relative emphasis has varied over time, from field to field,
and from country to country. Whatever the balance, doctoral
students contribute a significant proportion of the effort of research, and the opportunities for study and the direction and
content of their degree are influenced by the overall pattern of
research activity, funding, and organization.

The more utilitarian emphasis in the research role of higher
education has numerous implications for doctoral education.
Some impacts might be beneficial—the better opportunities for
industrially relevant experience and access to state-of-the-art
equipment that can arise from closer university-industry links
and broader funding bases, for example. Other effects pose
threats to the quality of doctoral education. The increasing concentration of research into special centers may well decrease
the commitment of faculty to their teaching role. In many
fields, research teams are becoming larger and roles more specialized. As a result, the quality of supervision may decline.
The relationship between graduate student and adviser is critical
at doctoral level. "Being treated as a junior colleague by the
adviser accounts for much of the variability in degree progress" (Girves and Wemmerus 1988, p. 185).

The current trends, however, may well operate against effective relationships and result in more exploitation of doctoral
students as a source of cheap labor. Students may be employed
on research projects, especially contract research, that are not
suitable for training future researchers. The selection of topics
for students' research may be overly influenced by the client's
needs and time scales. The skills acquired may be relatively

narrow, low-level technical skills rather than those needed by fully fledged professionals capable of undertaking independent research or contributing extensively to team projects (Clarke 1986; Kennedy 1982; Neumann and Lindsay 1988; Wofsy 1986).

At the level of system, another danger in the present trend in policy is that short-term goals may be overemphasized at the expense of long-term capability. A well-trained research work force requires time and skill to develop, whereas facilities and equipment, although important, can be acquired relatively easily and quickly by increasing expenditures. A focus on immediate output and benefits from research may thus impair the training of the next generation of researchers.

The whole face of graduate education is being altered by the increasing focus on vocationalism and utility. In addition to the clear redistribution in the fields of study, with growth being mainly concentrated in professional fields, a major shift has also occurred from Ph.D. training to specialized master's degrees (Glazer 1986). Increasing demand for advanced professional courses has been a worldwide trend, and, even at the doctoral level, the pattern of coursework and research for American Ph.D.s has been gaining in popularity over the research-only pattern (Blume 1986; Kyvik 1986; Lindsay 1986; Van Hout 1986). Although beyond the scope of this discussion, the form of training and the experience provided by the Ph.D. as preparation for both academic and other research careers are other topics needing thorough investigation (see, for example, Blume 1986; Woodring 1968; Zumeta 1982). A study of non-academic careers for Ph.D.s in the humanities found faculty indifference and even hostility to the notion and solitary, individualistic workstyles in students, negative attitudes toward business, and the belief that business rejects critical analysis (Risser 1982). Recommendations from the study included maintaining the rigor and substantive focus on Ph.D. training, permitting flexibility and cross-departmental courses, increasing opportunities for team learning, and emphasizing the need to meet deadlines.

In the sciences, the trend with a major impact on Ph.D. training is the movement of top-level research in some fields like physics out of the university and into national and even international research centers. It is clearly "a waste of talent not to use the best scientists as teachers and the best students as apprentices" (Kerr 1987, p. 193), so top-level training will

ave to follow. The full consequences of this relocation from
ae broad and supportive ethos of the university to the highly
pecialized and managed environment of the research institute
ave yet to be determined, but considerable care will have to
e exercised to avoid the dangers.

The challenge for doctoral education resides in the threat to
xcellence in research training that comes with the increasing
mphasis on utility in research. The trend carries potential ben-
fits for students, but they are also especially vulnerable in the
lash of the academic values of excellence and the commercial
alues of utility.

SUMMARY AND CONCLUSIONS

Notions of Excellence and Utility

Excellence and utility have always been central concepts in higher education, although their meaning and relative importance have changed over time. A long tradition in higher education regards excellence as a generalized and inherently valuable quality. From the classical and medieval views through the Humboldtian to the postwar disciplinary introversion, notions of excellence in higher education have tended to be self-justifying and hence rather divorced from human purposes. While excellence has been a central concern within the university, the periods of expansion and development in higher education have been directed by utilitarian considerations. Nevertheless, those universities that have flourished and served their societies well have been those engaged in the pursuit of excellence. Thus, while the utility of universities has at times resided in mastery of established dogmas, at others in cultivating minds and manners, and at others still in the discovery of new knowledge, universities without the quest for excellence have degenerated into arid diploma mills. When excellence is sought in activities that also have utility to society, higher education has prospered. Since 1945, the increasing importance of university research to economic goals has led to a greater emphasis on direct and immediate utility.

The organization of the university into disciplines with the resultant overspecialization and isolation of researchers also impedes problem-oriented research.

Other products of the postwar period have been the narrowing and divergence of the notions of excellence and utility. The expansion of basic research under government patronage reinforced the epistemological justification of research and led to an inward-looking, discipline-oriented, single-criterion view of excellence. With the economic decline in more recent years, the notion of utility became more restricted in focus and time. Essentially, the problem is that excellence has become too removed from human concerns and problems and that utility has become overly narrow and shortsighted. Excellence in research has come to be regarded as intrinsically good, separate from any other considerations, and utility is too often interpreted as having a customer waiting for the results. Efforts must be made to broaden the notions of excellence and utility and reestablish the harmony between them.

The setting for this endeavor is characterized by a number of trends. The notion of research has narrowed, differentiating it from "scholarship" through an emphasis on the "new" knowledge of the sciences. While research in the social sciences has been part of the successful partnership between government and science since the 1940s, some are concerned that within the current climate of fiscal and social upheaval, social science will become a less central part of the overall effort in research (Kraut and Duffy 1984). Certainly, priority has shifted to the natural sciences, and research is increasingly concentrated in large teams and centers. Closer links with industry have been developed and the proportion of applied research increased. These trends have contributed to a weakening of the teaching-research nexus.

In policy making, the current events reflect a "general spirit of hard instrumentalism" (Blume 1986, p. 217). In relationships with government, bureaucratization and control have increased, and institutions of higher education, particularly the research universities, have become corporate structures requiring careful management (Best 1988; Elzinga 1985). Nevertheless, effective steps can be taken to reduce bureaucracy and administrative cost, as the Florida demonstration project confirmed. In that project, the Florida state universities dropped administrative approvals for research projects funded by five federal agencies (Lewis 1988). To preserve the vigor and diversity of research, research sponsors and institutions should actively pursue more initiatives of this type.

Problems of the Narrow Notions of Excellence and Utility
The increasingly narrow concept of academic excellence focused on contribution to the discipline as the single criterion has led to increasing abstraction and specialization. With the growth of knowledge since World War II, the frontiers of science have become somewhat removed from the practical problems society experiences. Faculty have tended to concentrate on basic research and neglect practical problem solving. Nevertheless, major breakthroughs at the frontier of knowledge have often occurred through attempts to solve practical problems, and in any event an appropriate balance of research activity must be sought.

Narrow versions of utility are also damaging university research. While on the surface seeking greater utility for research in terms of maximizing its contribution to national economic goals is an unexceptionable policy, in its narrowest form it reduces the value of universities to society by overemphasizing one function at the expense of other valuable functions. Universities and their communities are connected in many ways. They make long-term social and cultural contributions as well as hort-term economic ones. Reducing basic research and down-grading the less obviously useful fields are not effective means of harnessing universities in the quest for economic recovery through applied research, development, and a revival in manufacturing. The situation and the problems are far too complex for simplistic solutions.

Utility in the form of "national needs" also has difficulties. While excellence is an internal criterion operating within the research community, national needs are likely to be politically defined within the interests and time scales of governments and industry. National priorities tend to be defined in narrowly utilitarian terms and with a short time scale in mind. In consequence, low-risk research with likely immediate benefits tends to be given preference over research with greater but longer-term potential. Research expertise is generally quite specialized and acquired over a long time period, however. The impact of particular research findings on society's problems may be substantial, but it often happens in a short time frame as the result of social, economic, or technological problems identified or confronted within the time spans of government policy. This mismatch of research and political time frames must be recognized and its consequences accepted if a pool of diverse research expertise is to be available at short notice (Muffo 1986).

The Way Forward

Harmonizing excellence and utility involves major challenges, both logistical and organizational. The failure of the university reward structure to provide incentives for public service is clearly one organizational barrier. The organization of the university into disciplines with the resultant overspecialization and isolation of researchers also impedes problem-oriented research (and increasingly basic research as well), which requires an integrated approach cutting across disciplinary boundaries. On the government side, the transient nature of political administrations, the frequent structural reorganizations and the short-term focus all hamper systematic university-based policy and problem-solving research (Dowling and Stumbo 1981).

Exclusive commitment to a discipline to the neglect of problem solving is at the heart of the conflict between excellence and utility. The difficulty is partly organizational and arises from the historical success of departments as the organizational basis for university research. Research in academic departments tends to be disciplinary, pure, and individual, while research in a center or institute tends to be more problem oriented, applied, multidisciplinary, and team based. Fostering this situation is the recognition and reward structure, which is believed to favor the former approach (Redner 1987, p. 56). Nevertheless, at least one study found no difference in career mobility for faculty clearly identified with interdisciplinary research, so the prospect for changing the bias toward disciplinary work might exist (Sams 1975). To foster the multidisciplinary approaches required for solving the problems of society, departmental influences will have to be counterbalanced.

The increasing levels of university-industry collaboration may already be affecting traditional orientations. A recent comparison of the NSF university-industry cooperative research programs showed striking and unexpected differences between projects and centers (Gray, Johnson, and Gidley 1986). Projects were generally found to involve cooperation over about a two-year period between an individual university researcher and a single company, while centers generally involved teams of researchers from several departments collaborating with representatives from several member companies in a more permanent arrangement. The university and industry participants in each type of venture held similar views about the rank order of goals, but a comparison between projects and centers revealed an almost complete reversal of priorities. In a list of seven goals, "patentable products" and "commercialized products" were ranked 1 and 2 by project respondents but 6 and 7 by center respondents, while "general expansion of knowledge" was ranked 7 for projects but 1 for centers.

A trend to be encouraged and exploited is the blurring of the boundaries between basic and applied research, a consequence of the direction of development in science and technology and the changing pattern of government and industry support (OECD 1982, p. 141). In the United States, recognition has been greater than elsewhere that it is the major research universities that can have most impact on industrial and technological problems, rather than the more vocationally oriented institutions (Shattock 1986). In any event, the categorization of research as pure or applied, or as mission-oriented or discipline-based, is rather arbitrary and artificial. It is questionable whether faculty view their research in terms of such polar opposites. Rather, research that is judged as excellent in its usefulness in furthering the discipline is often also potentially useful in social or economic terms. Where one dimension stops and another starts s not easily determined. It may be largely a matter of time, with research labeled "applied" having shorter-term utility than "basic" research. According to Churchman (1982), all research should be "basic" in that it should try to discover reality and "applied" in trying to respond to the most practical problem of all: how to design our lives.

Because all research should be concerned with human welfare, funding decisions should not be solely in the hands of the most immediate peer group of fellow researchers. More broadly based review committees, comprised of researchers from the range of disciplines broadly relevant to the research problems involved, have an important part to play. Their role should be to ensure that excellence is not judged in narrow terms, that the social and economic implications are considered, and that ethical and safety standards are maintained. Even universitywide panels could play a part in it as well as in strengthening academia's currently rather fragile sense of collegiality. It is time for university researchers, as a collegial body, to take greater responsibility for both the excellence and utility of their work.

Nor should national decisions be made by a single interest group. National needs and priorities should be determined through wide debate across the interest groups—governments, business, industry, the service sectors, community organizations, and higher education. The need exists for dialogue about the social value of research (Lepkowski 1982). The desirable balance between the service role and the traditional roles of research and teaching is a fundamental issue for debate, as is the ethical dimension of the service role: how to ensure the university encourages a balanced representation of competing interests and that private economic considerations do not bias the generation of knowledge (Dowling and Stumbo 1981).

Closer university-industry relationships are a primary way of increasing the utility of university research. Care must be taken, however, to respect the very different cultures and priorities involved (Cilley et al. 1986; Slaughter 1988). Proposals to develop closer relationships by making universities more like industrial firms or vice versa are neither conceptually sound nor feasible (Baer 1980). While one of the major challenges to the effective transfer of technology is the crossing of these cultural barriers, the very successful "culture of research" developed by the research universities must not be jeopardized by devaluing departmental organization and the teaching-research nexus in the pursuit of "new" structures. For example, the university's flexibility and rapid response to emerging research problems derive in large part from the flow of graduate students, allowing a more rapid redeployment than would a fully permanent staff (Committee of Vice Chancellors 1986, pp. 13–14).

Nevertheless, to span the growing gap between the frontiers of knowledge and society's practical problems, we need new flexible approaches and forms of organization. More problem-oriented centers within disciplinary departments are one possibility; another is to create new units linked with basic disciplines but oriented toward social problems. The mission of existing disciplinary departments could also be reoriented, provided the reward structure is modified appropriately. To do so requires a broadening of our notion of excellence by reassimilating a concern for utility. Institutional managers must be given the discretionary resources to encourage this process (Schuh 1986).

Summary of Recommendations

Achieving greater harmony between excellence and utility in the research role of universities is the responsibility of all involved, particularly faculty in the various disciplines, institutional leaders and administrators, higher education policy makers, and the sponsors and users of research—the government, business, and service sectors. The current trends in policy offer many opportunities, but detrimental effects result from a narrowing of the notions of excellence and utility, a narrowing of the notion of "research" to differentiate it from "scholarship," an undermining of the university's research culture, and a weakening of the teaching-research nexus.

The action required to counter these trends and achieve greater harmony between excellence and utility can be summarized in the following set of recommendations:

1. Harmonizing excellence and utility

Criteria of both excellence and utility should be incorporated into the assessment of research proposals by considering a range of potential contributions, including those to knowledge in the field, research methodology, practical social and economic problems, development of the researcher, teaching, and graduate training. Determined efforts must be made to counter the narrow notions of excellence associated with increasing abstraction, specialization, and isolation of research from human concerns, relevant practical problems, and even from the re-

earch in related fields. Narrow notions of utility concerned
only with immediate, short-term economic benefits must also
be rejected.

2. A broad view of "research"

Attempts to separate "research" from "scholarship" by emphasizing "new" knowledge and devaluing critical and integra-
tive work are antithetical to the basic nature of the university
and its role in advancing and preserving knowledge and so
should be strongly resisted.

3. The distinction between basic and applied research

The arbitrary and counterproductive tendency to regard the
distinction between basic and applied as a dichotomous one
should be rejected in favor of a holistic view that looks for
both "basic" and "applied" components in all research.

4. Balance and spread of research

Similarly, the broad range of approaches to research and disciplinary perspectives should be maintained, without reductions
of support for fields whose utility is less immediately apparent—the humanities, most social sciences, and the more abstract natural sciences.

5. Broadened panel membership

Peer review is fundamental to the systematic advancement of
knowledge, and judgments about research should remain in the
hands of those best able to judge the excellence of research rec-
ords and proposals. Research review panels should not be restricted to the most immediate peer group of fellow researchers,
however, but should include researchers from related fields and
in some cases representatives from each of the broad field
groupings—the humanities, the social sciences, and the natural
sciences.

6. Conflict of interest

Researchers with substantial commercial interests in a research topic should not participate in judging proposals.

7. University responsiveness

Institutions should seek to balance competing interests in
dealing with their constituencies and ensure that short-term
commercial considerations are not given undue weight.

8. Reward structure

Institutional reward structures should be revised to reflect the full range of contributions a faculty member can make.

9. Organizational diversity

Organizational diversity and flexibility, which together with the multiplicity of research funding sources distinguish American higher education from the other OECD countries, should be strengthened as a barrier against bureaucratization, a reluctance to take risks, and the application of undue political and economic pressures. The frontiers of knowledge and society's problems must be linked through new approaches and forms of organization, but traditional disciplinary departments and individual researchers should not be deprived of resources to support multidisciplinary centers and large research teams.

10. Collegiality

The research community should develop a greater collegial responsibility for the overall research enterprise in terms of standards of excellence, the assessment of social and economic implications, and the adherence to ethical and safety standards.

11. Consultation on national needs

National needs and priorities should be determined through wide consultation and debate among the interest groups—researchers, universities, governments, and the business and service sectors.

12. Preserving the "research culture"

In developing better relationships with industry and in improving the transfer of technology, the very effective research culture of American universities must not be undermined. The benefits of the disciplinary and departmental structures and the teaching-research nexus should not be forgotten in the search for ways to improve technology transfer and the commercialization of research findings.

13. The teaching-research nexus

The continual updating of course content and a critical orientation toward knowledge are the main benefits of the teaching-research nexus. The emphasis on research and greater utility must not be allowed to divorce university teaching, at either the undergraduate or graduate level, from its source—critical in-

¡uiry. While graduate students can benefit from industrially ¡elevant experience and state-of-the-art equipment, exploita-¡on and neglect are also possible outcomes of current trends. ¡raduate students are especially vulnerable in the clash of the ¡cademic values of excellence and the commercial values ¡f utility.

14. A pool of researchers

Regardless of current priorities, a pool of researchers should ¡e maintained in each field in recognition of the time required ¡o develop research capability and international leadership, ¡ompared to the time in which social, economic, and techno-¡ogical problems emerge.

All the recommendations are generally relevant for the four ¡ain constituencies of the university research system. In terms ¡f responsibility for putting the recommendations into effect, ¡owever, some recommendations have specific relevance for ¡articular constituencies. The appropriate responsibilities for ¡mplementation are identified in table 1.

TABLE 1
RESPONSIBILITIES FOR IMPLEMENTATION

	Constituency			
	Faculty	*Institutions*	*Policy Makers*	*Sponsors*
1. Harmonizing excellence and utility	x	x	x	x
2. A broad view of "research"	x	x	x	x
3. The distinction between basic and applied research	x	x	x	x
4. Balance and spread of research		x	x	x
5. Broadened panel membership		x		x
6. Conflict of interest		x		x
7. University responsiveness		x		
8. Reward structure		x		
9. Organizational diversity		x	x	x
10. Collegiality	x	x		
11. Consultation on national needs			x	x
12. Preserving the "research culture"		x	x	x
13. The teaching-research nexus	x	x		
14. A pool of researchers		x	x	x

Concluding Comments

While all those involved in university research have a part to play in harmonizing excellence and utility in research, the heaviest responsibility falls upon institutional leaders. The national nature of some of the problems and the growth of government regulation cannot provide an excuse for lack of institutional initiative. The decentralized American higher education system allows institutions with good leadership and effective management to position themselves within the system according to their history, circumstances, and aspirations (Best 1988; Geiger 1985a; Volkwein 1987). Future needs will be ill served by narrow interpretations of utility and the downgrading of excellence but well served by harmonizing the two in the pursuit of excellence in serving society. Research policy should be directed toward maintaining diversity, flexibility, and an appropriate balance of the different fields and types of research. Our higher education institutions can and must meet the challenge of excellence *and* utility.

REFERENCES

The Educational Resources Information Center (ERIC) Clearinghouse
on Higher Education abstracts and indexes the current literature on
higher education for inclusion in ERIC's data base and announcement
in ERIC's monthly bibliographic journal, *Resources in Education*
(RIE). Most of these publications are available through the ERIC
Document Reproduction Service (EDRS). For publications cited in this
bibliography that are available from EDRS, ordering number and price
code are included. Readers who wish to order a publication should
write to the ERIC Document Reproduction Service, 3900 Wheeler
Avenue, Alexandria, Virginia 22304. (Phone orders with VISA or
MasterCard are taken at 800/227-ERIC or 703/823-0500.) When
ordering, please specify the document (ED) number. Documents are
available as noted in microfiche (MF) and paper copy (PC). If you
have the price code ready when you call EDRS, an exact price can be
quoted. The last page of the latest issue of *Resources in Education*
also has the current cost, listed by code.

'Academic R&D Shows Moderate Growth.'' 1982. *Chemical and
Engineering News* 60(30): 68–71.

Advisory Board for the Research Councils. May 1987. *A Strategy for
the Science Base*. A discussion paper prepared for the Secretary of
State for Education and Science. London: Her Majesty's Stationery
Office.

Andren, Carl G. 1982. "Higher Education and Research as Dynamics
for the Development of Society." In *The Universities in a Changing
World: Adaptation or Guidance?* edited by Charles H. Belanger.
Proceedings of the European Association for Institutional Research
Forum, 25–27 August, Uppsala, Sweden. ED 251 002. 166 pp.
MF–01; PC–07.

Ashby, Eric. 1967. "The Future of the Nineteenth Century Idea of a
University." *Minerva* 6(1): 3–17.

Astin, A.W. 1980. "When Does a College Deserve to Be Called High
Quality?" *Current Issues in Higher Education* 2(1): 1–9.

———. 1985. *Achieving Educational Excellence*. San Francisco:
Jossey-Bass.

Atelsek, Frank J., and Irene L. Gomberg. January 1976. "Faculty
Research: Level of Activity and Choice of Area." American
Council on Education Higher Education Panel Report No. 29. ED
119 589. 38 pp. MF–01; PC–02.

Australian Science and Technology Council. 1987. *Improving the
Research Performance of Australia's Universities and Other Higher
Education Institutions*. A report to the prime minister by the Aus-
tralian Science and Technology Council. Canberra: Commonwealth
Government Printer.

Baer, Walter S. January 1980. "Strengthening University-Industry
Interactions." ED 190 033. 34 pp. MF–01; PC–02.

Barber, Albert A. 1985. "University-Industry Research Cooperation." *Journal of the Society of Research Administrators* 17(2): 19–30.

Bassis, Michael S., and Alan E. Guskin. 1986. "Building Quality: Research and the Regional Institutions." *Change* 18(4): 57–60 + .

Becher, Tony. 1981. "Toward a Definition of Disciplinary Cultures." *Studies in Higher Education* 6(2): 109–22.

———. 1987a. "Disciplinary Discourse." *Studies in Higher Education* 12(3): 261–74.

———. 1987b. "The Disciplinary Shaping of the Profession." In *The Academic Profession*, edited by Burton R. Clark. Berkeley: Univ. of California Press.

Becher, Tony, and Maurice Kogan. 1980. *Process and Structure in Higher Education*. London: Heinemann.

Ben-David, Joseph. 1977. *Centers of Learning: Britain, France, Germany, United States.* New York: McGraw-Hill.

Best, John H. 1988. "The Revolution of Markets and Management: Toward a History of American Higher Education since 1945." *Journal of Higher Education* 28(2): 177–98.

Biglan, Anthony. 1973a. "The Characteristics of Subject Matter in Different Academic Areas." *Journal of Applied Psychology* 57(3): 195–203.

———. 1973b. "Relationships between Subject Matter Characteristics and the Structure and Output of University Departments." *Journal of Applied Psychology* 57(3): 204–13.

Bloom, Allan. 1987. *The Closing of the American Mind: How Higher Education Has Failed Democracy and Impoverished the Souls of Today's Students.* New York: Simon & Schuster.

Blume, Stuart S. 1982. "The Framework for Analysis." In *The Future of Research*, edited by Geoffrey Oldham. Guildford, Surrey: Society for Research into Higher Education.

———. 1986. "The Development and Current Dilemmas of Post-graduate Education." *European Journal of Education* 21(3): 217–22.

Bok, Derek. 1982. *Beyond the Ivory Tower: The Social Responsibilities of the Modern University.* Cambridge, Mass.: Harvard Univ. Press.

Booth, William. 6 January 1989. "NIH Scientists Agonize over Technology Transfer." *Science* 243: 20–21.

Botkin, James, Dan Dimancescu, and Ray Stata. 1982. *Global Stakes: The Future of High Technology in America.* Cambridge, Mass.: Ballinger.

Bowen, Howard R. 1977. *Investment in Learning.* San Francisco: Jossey-Bass.

Bowen, Howard R., and Jack H. Schuster. 1986. *American Professors: A National Resource Imperiled.* New York: Oxford Univ. Press.

Bowen, James. 1978. "The Problem of Excellence or Equality in Education: A Historical Overview." In *Excellence or Equality: Dilemmas for Policy and Planning in Australian Higher Education*, edited by Peter R. Chippendale and Paula V. Wilkes. Toowoomba, Queensland: Darling Downs Institute of Advanced Education.

Boyer, Carol M., and Darrell R. Lewis. 1985. *And on the Seventh Day: Faculty Consulting and Supplemental Income.* ASHE-ERIC Higher Education Report No. 3. Washington, D.C.: Association for the Study of Higher Education. ED 262 743. 89 pp. MF–01; PC–04.

Breslin, Janice. June 1986. "State Initiatives to Promote Technological Innovation and Economic Growth." Maryland State Board for Higher Education Postsecondary Education Research Report. ED 270 047. 62 pp. MF–01; PC–03.

Brickman, Ronald. 1985. "The University Research System: Policies, Performance, and Paradoxes." In *The University Research System: The Public Policies of the Home of Scientists*, edited by Bjorn Wittrock and Aant Elzinga. Stockholm: Almqvist & Wiksell International.

Brown, Leslie M. 1978. "Excellence or Equality: A Dilemma in the Philosophy of Education?" In *Excellence or Equality: Dilemmas for Policy and Planning in Australian Higher Education*, edited by Peter R. Chippendale and Paula V. Wilkes. Toowoomba, Queensland: Darling Downs Institute of Advanced Education.

Brown, Theodore L. 1985. "University-Industry Relations: Is There a Conflict?" *Journal of the Society of Research Administrators* 17(2): 7–17.

Brubacher, John S. 1977. *On the Philosophy of Higher Education.* San Francisco: Jossey-Bass.

Brubacher, John S., and Willis Rudy. 1968. *Higher Education in Transition: A History of American Colleges and Universities, 1636–1968.* New York: Harper & Row.

Burgess, Tyrell. 1978. "Excellence or Equality: A Dilemma for Higher Education." In *Excellence or Equality: Dilemmas for Policy and Planning in Australian Higher Education*, edited by Peter R. Chippendale and Paula V. Wilkes. Toowoomba, Queensland: Darling Downs Institute of Advanced Education.

Burke, April. 1985. "University Policies on Conflict of Interest and Delay of Publication." *Journal of College and University Law* 12(2): 175–200.

Buxton, Thomas H., and Keith W. Prichard, eds. 1975. *Excellence in University Teaching.* Columbia: Univ. of South Carolina Press.

Carter, Charles. 1980. *Higher Education for the Future.* Oxford: Basil Blackwell.

"Changes in Government Policy that Would Help Colleges: 36 Experts' Recommendations." 4 September 1985. *Chronicle of Higher Education* 31(1): 56–60.

Churchman, C. West. 1982. "An Interdisciplinary Look at Science Policy in an Age of Decreased Funding." In *Research in the Age of the Steady-State University*, edited by Don I. Phillips and Benjamin S. Shen. American Association for the Advancement of Science Selected Symposium 60. Boulder, Colo.: Westview Press.

Cilley, Earl G., Thomas L. Tolbert, Harvard H. Hill, Jr., W.H. Selders, and David L. Keaton. 1986. "Industry Access to University Technology: Prospects and Problems." In *The Private Sector/University Technology Alliance: Making It Work*, edited by Earl J. Freise. Proceedings of a conference of the National Council of University Research Administrators, 4–7 September 1984, Dallas, Texas. ED 272 083. 250 pp. MF–01; PC–10.

Clark, Burton R. 1983. *The Higher Education System: Academic Organization in Cross-National Perspective.* Berkeley: Univ. of California Press.

————— , ed. 1984. *Perspectives on Higher Education: Eight Disciplinary and Comparative Views.* Berkeley: Univ. of California Press.

Clarke, Adrienne E. 1986. "Intellectual Property—Problems and Paradoxes." *Journal of Tertiary Educational Administration* 8(1): 13–26.

Cohen, M.D., and J.G. March. 1974. *Leadership and Ambiguity: The American College President.* New York: McGraw-Hill.

Cole, Stephen, Jonathan R. Cole, and Gary A. Simon. 1981. "Chance and Consensus in Peer Review." *Science* 214: 881–86.

Committee of Vice Chancellors and Principals. 1986. *The Future of the Universities.* London: Author.

Copi, Irving M. 1961. *Introduction to Logic.* New York: Macmillan.

Corcoran, Mary, and Shirley M. Clark. 1984. "Professional Socialization and Contemporary Career Attitudes of Three Faculty Generations." *Research in Higher Education* 20(2): 131–53.

Cragg, Wes. 1984. "Academic Freedom and Mission-Oriented Research Funding." *Interchange* 14–15(4–1): 148–50.

Creswell, John W. 1985. *Faculty Research Performance: Lessons from the Sciences and the Social Sciences.* ASHE-ERIC Higher Education Report No. 4. Washington, D.C.: Association for the Study of Higher Education. ED 267 677. 92 pp. MF–01; PC–04.

Crosson, Patricia H. 1983. *Public Service in Higher Education: Practices and Priorities.* ASHE-ERIC Higher Education Report No. 7. Washington, D.C.: Association for the Study of Higher Education. ED 239 569. 140 pp. MF–01; PC–06.

Cyert, Richard M., and Peggy A. Knapp. 1984. "Research in the Humanities." *Liberal Education* 70(2): 95–101.

Dawkins, John S. 1987. *Higher Education: A Policy Discussion Paper*. Canberra: Australian Government Publishing Service.

Dill, David D. 1982a. "The Management of Academic Culture: Notes on the Management of Meaning and Social Integration." *Higher Education* 11: 303–20.

————. 1982b. "The Structure of the Academic Profession: Toward a Definition of Ethical Issues." *Journal of Higher Education* 53(3): 255–67.

————. 1986. "Research as a Scholarly Activity: Context and Culture." In *Measuring Faculty Research Performance*, edited by John W. Creswell. New Directions for Institutional Research No. 50. San Francisco: Jossey-Bass.

Dowling, Noreen G., and Diana Stumbo. 1981. "Public Service Research at University of California–Davis." Paper presented at the annual meeting of the Rural Sociological Society, 20 August, Guelph, Canada. ED 209 986. 19 pp. MF–01; PC–01.

Elton, Lewis. 1986. "Research and Teaching: Symbiosis or Conflict." *Higher Education* 15: 299–304.

Elzinga, Aant. 1985. "Research, Bureaucracy, and the Drift of Epistemic Criteria." In *The University Research System: The Public Policies of the Home of Scientists*, edited by Bjorn Wittrock and Aant Elzinga. Stockholm: Almqvist & Wiksell International.

Feldman, Kenneth A. 1987. "Research Productivity and Scholarly Accomplishment of College Teachers as Related to Their Instructional Effectiveness: A Review and Exploration." *Research in Higher Education* 26(3): 227–98.

Fincher, Cameron. 1984. "Planning for Quality and Efficiency in Higher Education." In *Beyond Retrenchment: Planning for Quality and Efficiency*, edited by Charles H. Belanger. Proceedings of the European Association for Institutional Research, 21–24 August, Brussels, Belgium. ED 260 616. 148 pp. MF–01; PC–06.

Finkelstein, Martin J. 1984. *The American Academic Profession: A Synthesis of Social Scientific Inquiry since World War II*. Columbus: Ohio State Univ. Press.

Flexner, Abraham. 1967 (orig. pub. 1930). *Universities: American, English, German*. New York: Columbia Univ., Teachers College Press.

Flexner, Hans. 1979. "The Curriculum, the Disciplines, and Interdisciplinarity in Higher Education: Historical Perspective." In *Interdisciplinarity and Higher Education*, edited by Joseph J. Knockelmans. University Park: Pennsylvania State Univ. Press.

Flood-Page, Colin. 1973. "Teaching and Research: Happy Symbiosis or Hidden Warfare?" *Vestes: The Australian Universities Review* 16(2): 188–201.

Folger, John. 1984. "Assessment of Quality for Accountability." In *Financial Incentives for Academic Quality*, edited by John Folger.

New Directions for Higher Education No. 48. San Francisco: Jossey-Bass.

Ford Foundation. 1977. *Research Universities and the National Interest.* Report from Fifteen University Presidents. New York: Author.

Friedrich, Robert J., and Stanley J. Michalak. 1983. "Why Doesn't Research Improve Teaching?" *Journal of Higher Education* 54(2): 145–63.

Gardner, John. 1961. *Excellence: Can We Be Equal and Excellent Too?* New York: Harper & Row.

Gaston, J. 1978. *The Reward System in British and American Science.* New York: John Wiley & Sons.

Gaziel, Haim. 1980. "Advisory Councils in a Centralised Educational System: A Case Study from France." *European Journal of Education* 15(4): 399–407.

Geiger, Roger L. 1985a. "Hierarchy and Diversity in American Research Universities." In *The University Research System: The Public Policies of the Home of Scientists*, edited by Bjorn Wittrock and Aant Elzinga. Stockholm: Almqvist & Wiksell International.

———. 1985b. "The Home of Scientists: A Perspective on University Research." In *The University Research System: The Public Policies of the Home of Scientists*, edited by Bjorn Wittrock and Aant Elzinga. Stockholm: Almqvist & Wiksell International.

Girves, Jean E., and Virginia Wemmerus. 1988. "Developing Models of Graduate Student Degree Progress." *Journal of Higher Education* 59(2): 163–89.

Glazer, Judith S. 1986. *The Master's Degree: Tradition, Diversity, Innovation.* ASHE-ERIC Higher Education Report No. 6. Washington, D.C.: Association for the Study of Higher Education. ED 279 260. 142 pp. MF–01; PC–06.

Gray, Denis, Elmima C. Johnson, and Teresa R. Gidley. 1986. "Industry-University Projects and Centers: An Empirical Comparison of Two Federally Funded Models of Cooperative Science." *Evaluation Review* 10(6): 776–93.

Haneman, Vincent S. 1975. "Faculty Research and Undergraduate Instruction." *Engineering Education* 65(6): 450–51.

Johnson, Lynn G. 1984. *The High-Technology Connection: Academic/Industrial Cooperation for Economic Growth.* ASHE-ERIC Higher Education Report No. 6. Washington, D.C.: Association for the Study of Higher Education. ED 255 130. 129 pp. MF–01; PC–06.

Jones, Denis. 1984. "Budgeting for Academic Quality: Structures and Strategies." In *Financial Incentives for Academic Quality*, edited by John Folger. New Directions for Higher Education No. 48. San Francisco: Jossey-Bass.

Kennedy, David. 1982. "Kennedy: Future Academic Research Policy." *Chemical and Engineering News* 60(29): 35–40.

Kerr, Clark. 1972 (orig. pub. 1963). *The Uses of the University: With a "Postscript—1972."* Cambridge, Mass.: Harvard Univ. Press.

———. 1987. "A Critical Age in the University World: Accumulated Heritage versus Modern Imperatives." *European Journal of Education* 22(2): 183–93.

Knight, Randall D. 1987. "Science, Space, and Scholarship: University Research and the Strategic Defense Initiative." Paper presented at the ASHE annual meeting, February. ED 281 444. 26 pp. MF–01; PC–02.

Kraut, Alan G., and Sarah W. Duffy. 1984. "Academics, Science, Public Policy: A Coalition for the 1980s." *American Psychologist* 39(9): 1043–44.

Kruh, Robert F. 1982. "An Assessment of Research Doctorate Programs in the United States." In *Graduate Education: An Investment in Knowledge.* Proceedings of the annual meeting of the Council of Graduate Schools in the United States, 1–2 December, Colorado Springs, Colorado. ED 239 579. 207 pp. MF–01; PC–09.

Kyvik, Svein. 1986. "Postgraduate Education in Norway." *European Journal of Education* 21(3): 251–60.

Lawrence, Judith K., and Kenneth C. Green. 1980. *A Question of Quality: The Higher Education Ratings Game.* AAHE-ERIC Higher Education Report No. 5. Washington D.C.: American Association for Higher Education. ED 192 667. 76 pp. MF–01; PC–04.

Lepkowski, Wil. 1982. "Public Concern: New Force in Science Policy." *Chemical and Engineering News* 60(19): 43–44.

———. 1984. "House Committee Sets Agenda for Huge Science Policy Study." *Chemical and Engineering News* 62(43): 16–19.

Leverhulme Report. 1983. *Excellence in Diversity: Toward a New Strategy for Higher Education.* Guildford, Surrey: Society for Research into Higher Education.

Lewis, James P. 1988. "Research Administration: The Cost in Dollars and Faculty Time." *Journal of the Society of Research Administrators* 19(3): 39–46.

Lindsay, Alan W. 1982. "Institutional Performance in Higher Education: The Efficiency Dimension." *Review of Educational Research* 52(2): 175–99.

———. 1986. "Doctoral Education: Continuity and Change." In *The Learner in Higher Education: A Forgotten Species?* edited by Allen Miller and Gerlese Sache-Akerlind. *Research and Development in Higher Education* (9). Sydney: Higher Education Research and Development Society of Australasia.

Lindsay, Alan, and Ruth Neumann. 1987. "University Research in Flux: Policy Debate in Australia." *Higher Education* 16(4): 433–48.

Lynton, Ernest A., and Sandra E. Elman. 1987. *New Priorities for the*

University: Meeting Society's Needs for Applied Knowledge and Competent Individuals. San Francisco: Jossey-Bass.

McGrath, Earl J. 1962. "Characteristics of Outstanding College Teachers." *Journal of Higher Education* 33(3): 148–52.

Martin, Ben R., and John Irvine with Nigel Minchin. 1986. *An International Comparison of Government Funding of Academic and Academically Related Research.* ABRC Science Policy Studies No. 2. Brighton, Sussex: Univ. of Sussex, Science Policy Research Unit.

Mayhew, Lewis B. March 1973. "The Role of Research in California Higher Education." ED 076 122. 81 pp. MF–01; PC–04.

Merton, Robert K. 1973. *The Sociology of Science: Theoretical and Empirical Investigations,* edited with an introduction by Norman W. Storer. Chicago: Univ. of Chicago Press.

Michalak, Stanley J., and Robert J. Friedrich. 1981. "Research Productivity and Teaching Effectiveness at a Small Liberal Arts College." *Journal of Higher Education* 52(6): 578–97.

Miller, Howard S. 1970. *Dollars for Research: Science and Its Patrons in Nineteenth Century America.* Seattle: Univ. of Washington Press.

Muffo, John A. 1986. "The Impact of Faculty Research on State and Federal Policy." In *Measuring Faculty Research Performance,* edited by John W. Creswell. New Directions for Institutional Research No. 50. San Francisco: Jossey-Bass.

Muir, William R. 1987a. "The Historical Development of the Teacher-Research Ideal in Germany and the U.S.A." Paper presented at the ASHE annual meeting, February. ED 281 435. 55 pp. MF–01; PC–03.

———. 1987b. "The Structure of the Academic Dogma: Ancient History Is Not Just Academic." Paper presented at the ASHE annual meeting, February. ED 281 434. 24 pp. MF–01; PC–01.

National Commission on Research. August 1980. "Research Personnel: An Essay on Policy." ED 201 216. 17 pp. MF–01; PC–01.

Neumann, Ruth, and Alan Lindsay. 1987. "Excellence at Risk? The Future of Research and Research Training in Australian Universities." *Australian Quarterly* 59(2): 199–209.

———. 1988. "Research Policy and the Changing Nature of Australia's Universities." *Higher Education* 17(3): 307–21.

Newman, John Henry. 1960 (based on text of 1899 impression). *The Idea of a University: Defined and Illustrated in Nine Discourses Delivered to the Catholics of Dublin in Occasional Lectures and Essays Addressed to the Members of the Catholic University,* edited with an introduction and notes by Martin J. Svaglic. San Francisco: Rinehart Press.

Omenn, Gilbert S., and Denis J. Prager. 1982. "Research Universities and the Future: Challenges and Opportunities." In *Research in the Age of the Steady-State University*, edited by Don I. Phillips and Benjamin S. Shen. American Association for the Advancement of Science Selected Symposium 60. Boulder, Colo.: Westview Press.

Organisation for Economic Cooperation and Development. 1980. *Technical Change and Economic Policy: Science and Technology in the New Economic and Social Context*. Paris: Author.

―――. 1981. *The Future of University Research*. Paris: Author. ED 208 793. 79 pp. MF–01; PC not available EDRS.

―――. 1982. *The University and the Community: The Problems of Changing Relationships*. Centre for Educational Research and Innovation. Paris: Author. ED 244 353. 157 pp. MF–01; PC not available EDRS.

―――. 1987. *Universities under Scrutiny*. Paris: Author.

Pelz, Donald C., and Frank M. Andrews. 1966. *Scientists in Organizations: Productive Climates for Research and Development*. New York: John Wiley & Sons.

Peters, Thomas J., and Robert H. Waterman. 1982. *In Search of Excellence*. New York: Harper & Row.

Phillips, Don I. 1982. "Introduction: The Future of Academic Research." In *Research in the Age of the Steady-State University*, edited by Don I. Phillips and Benjamin S. Shen. American Association for the Advancement of Science Selected Symposium 60. Boulder, Colo.: Westview Press.

Phillips, Don I., and Benjamin S.P. Shen, eds. 1982. *Research in the Age of the Steady-State University*. American Association for the Advancement of Science Selected Symposium 60, Boulder, Colo.: Westview Press.

Prager, Denis. 1984. "Trends in Government and Academic Institutions Affecting Science." *American Psychologist* 39(9): 1056–59.

Premfors, Rune. 1982. "Values and Value Tradeoffs in Higher Education Policy." *Policy Sciences* 14(4): 365–78.

Press, Frank. 1982. "Rethinking Science Policy." *Science* 218(4567): 28–30.

Redner, Harry. 1987. "The Institutionalization of Science: A Critical Synthesis." *Social Epistemology* 1(1): 37–59.

Ringer, Fritz K. 1969. *The Decline of the German Mandarins: The German Academic Community, 1890–1933*. Cambridge, Mass.: Harvard Univ. Press.

Risser, Nancy. 1982. "Graduate Education in the Humanities: Some Options for the Future." In *Graduate Education: An Investment in Knowledge*. Proceedings of the annual meeting of the Council of Graduate Schools in the United States, 1–2 December, Colorado Springs, Colorado. ED 239 579. 207 pp. MF–01; PC–09.

Rosenzweig, Robert M., and Barbara Turlington. 1982. *The Research Universities and Their Patrons*. Berkeley: Univ. of California.

Ross, Murray G. 1967. "The University and Community Service." Paper delivered at the annual meeting of the Association of Universities and Colleges of Canada, 30 October–3 November, Montreal, Quebec, Canada. ED 017 866. 35 pp. MF–01; PC–02.

Ruscio, Kenneth P. 1987. "The Distinctive Scholarship of the Selective Liberal Arts College." *Journal of Higher Education* 58(2): 203–22.

Sams, Henry W. March 1975. "The Academic Administration of Research: A Descriptive Analysis." ED 144 506. 302 pp. MF–01; PC–13.

Schuh, G. Edward. 1986. "Revitalizing the Land-Grant University: An Abridgment." Paper presented at a faculty seminar of the College of Agriculture "Year of the Scholar" Lecture Series No. 1, 2 October, Columbus, Ohio. ED 282 473. 28 pp. MF–01; PC–02.

Schwartzman, Simon. 1984. "The Focus on Scientific Activity." In *Perspectives on Higher Education: Eight Disciplinary and Comparative Views*, edited by Burton R. Clark. Berkeley: Univ. of California Press.

Scott, Peter. 1984. *The Crisis of the University*. London: Croom Helm.

Scurla, Herbert. 1984. *Wilhelm v. Humboldt: Reformator-Wissenschaftler-Philosoph*. Munich: Wilhelm Heyne Verlag.

Shattock, Michael. 1986. "False Images but a Renewed Promise." In *Beyond the Limelight*, edited by Stuart Bosworth. Essays on the Occasion of the Silver Jubilee of the Conference of University Administrators. Salford: Conference of University Administrators, Univ. of Salford.

Slaughter, Sheila. 1988. "Academic Freedom and the State." *Journal of Higher Education* 59(3): 241–62.

Smith, Stuart L. 1982. "The Changing Role of Universities." In *The Universities in a Changing World: Adaptation or Guidance?* edited by Charles H. Belanger. Proceedings of the European Association for Institutional Research Forum, 25–27 August, Uppsala, Sweden. ED 251 002. 166 pp. MF–01; PC–07.

Standing Conference of Rectors and Vice Chancellors of the European Universities (Geneva, Switzerland). 1964. "The Optimum and Maximum Size of the University." ED 072 762. 336 pp. MF–01; PC–14.

Stecklein, John E. 1982. "Changes in Faculty Characteristics, Activities, and Attitudes over Twenty-Five Years at a Major United States University." In *The Universities in a Changing World: Adaptation or Guidance?* edited by Charles H. Belanger. Proceedings of the European Association for Institutional Research Forum, 25–27 August, Uppsala, Sweden. ED 251 002. 166 pp. MF–01; PC–07.

Stone, Lawrence. 1983. "Social Control and Intellectual Excellence:

Oxbridge and Edinburgh, 1560–1983." In *Universities, Society, and the Future*, edited by Nicholas Phillipson. Edinburgh: Univ. of Edinburgh Press.

Strike, Kenneth A. 1985. "Is There a Conflict between Equity and Excellence?" *Educational Evaluation and Policy Analysis* 7(4): 409–16.

Tamas, Pal. 1980. "Policies for Science and for Education: Conflicts and Contacts." *European Journal of Education* 15(4): 363–75.

Tierney, William G. 1988. "Organizational Culture in Higher Education." *Journal of Higher Education* 59(1): 1–21.

Tolbert, T.L. 1985. "Industry/University Research Cooperation. Convenience or Necessity: The Industrial View." *Journal of the Society of Research Administrators* 17(2): 45–52.

Turner, R. Steven. 1971. "The Growth of Professorial Research in Prussia, 1818–1848: Causes and Context." *Historical Studies in the Physical Sciences* 3: 137–82.

———. 1974. "University Reformers and Professorial Scholarship in Germany, 1760–1806." In *The University in Society*, vol. 2, edited by Lawrence Stone. Princeton: Princeton Univ. Press.

Van Hout, Johannes. 1986. "Toward a New Structure for Postgraduate Research Training in the Netherlands." *European Journal of Education* 21(3): 275–86.

Veblen, Thorstein. 1969 (orig. pub. 1918). *The Higher Learning in America: A Memorandum on the Conduct of Universities by Businessmen.* New York: W.B. Huebsch.

Veysey, Laurence R. 1965. *The Emergence of the American University.* Chicago: Univ. of Chicago Press.

Volkwein, J. Fredericks. 1987. "Measuring the Benefits of University Autonomy from State Regulation." Paper presented at the ASHE annual meeting, February. ED 281 433. 28 pp. MF–01; PC–02.

Ward, Wilfrid. 1915. *Introduction to Cardinal John Henry Newman on the Scope and Nature of University Education.* London: J.M. Dent & Sons.

West, J.F. 1965. *The Great Intellectual Revolution.* London: John Murray.

White, Donald J. 1982. "Investing in Graduate Education: Who Invests? Who Benefits?" In *Graduate Education: An Investment in Knowledge.* Proceedings of the annual meeting of the Council of Graduate Schools in the United States, 1–2 December, Colorado Springs, Colorado. ED 239 579. 207 pp. MF–01; PC–09.

Wikstron, J. 1982. "Guidance and Adaptation in Higher Education and Research—Some Swedish Experience." In *The Universities in a Changing World—Adaptation or Guidance?* edited by Charles H. Belanger. Proceedings of the European Association for Institutional Research Forum, 25–27 August, Uppsala, Sweden. ED 251 002. 166 pp. MF–01; PC–07.

Williams, Gareth. 1984. "Research and Research Policy." *Higher Education in Europe* 9(4): 11–16.

Williams, Gareth, and T. Blackstone. 1983. "Marriage of Convenience between Research and Teaching." In *Response to Adversity.* Leverhulme Programme Report No. 10. Guildford, Surrey: Society for Research into Higher Education.

Wittrock, Bjorn. 1985a. "Before the Dawn. . .Humanism and Technocracy University Research Policy." In *The University Research System: The Public Policies of the Home of Scientists,* edited by Bjorn Wittrock and Aant Elzinga. Stockholm: Almqvist & Wiksell International.

———. 1985b. "Dinosaurs or Dolphins? Rise and Resurgence of the Research-Oriented University." In *The University Research System: The Public Policies of the Home of Scientists,* edited by Bjorn Wittrock and Aant Elzinga. Stockholm: Almqvist & Wiksell International.

Wittrock, Bjorn, and Aant Elzinga, eds. 1985. *The University Research System: The Public Policies of the Home of Scientists.* Stockholm: Almqvist & Wiksell International.

Wofsy, Leon. 1986. "Biotechnology and the University." *Journal of Higher Education* 57(5): 477–92.

Woodring, Paul. 1968. *The Higher Learning in America: A Reassessment.* New York: McGraw-Hill.

Zollinger, Richard. 1982. "State-Sponsored Research: Cooperation or Conflict?" *Educational Record* 63(2): 4–9.

Zumeta, William. 1982. "Doctoral Program and the Labor Market, or How Should We Respond to the 'Ph.D. Glut'?" *Higher Education* 11(3): 321–43.

INDEX

A

Academic disciplines
 academic culture, 33–34
 funding differences, 6–7
 introversion, 71
 research orientation, 32–33
 "utilitarian," 26
 values, 43
Access to education, 49
Applied research, 4, 57, 74, 75, 77
Aristotle, 14, 23
Aristotelian thought, 19, 20
Arts funding, 6

B

Bacon, Francis, 20
Basic research
 funding, 51
 reduced, 73
 vs. applied, 4, 57, 74, 75, 77
Biology: research values, 34
Biotechnology
 conflict of interest, 62
 military/industrial interest, 7
British Advisory Board for the Research Councils, 6
British universities, 38, 39, 47
Bush, Vannevar, 49

C

Cambridge University, 15
Catholic University (Dublin), 23, 24
Collegiality, 78
Commercial interests, 62
Conflict of interest
 avoidance, 77
 industry support, 9
 peer review, 62
 university policy, 52
Content view of excellence, 15
Council of Graduate Schools, 41
Curriculum
 debates, 25–27
 relationship to research and knowledge, 37

D

Decentralization benefits, 80

The Challenge for Research in Higher Education

J

Japan: R&D fnding, 5, 6

Johns Hopkins University, 16, 24

K

Knowledge
      groupings, 36, 38–39
      link to excellence, 48
      "new," 21, 37, 71, 77
      preservation and teaching, 19–20
      relationship to research and curriculum, 37
      search for new, 38

L

Land-grant universities
      American innovation, 25
      service role, 47, 52

Lehrfreit, 22

Lernfreiheit, 22

Liberal education, 23

Library services, 42–43

Life sciences funding, 6, 7

M

Medieval universities, 19–20, 45

Master's degrees, 68

Mathematical sciences funding, 7

Military research funding, 6, 34

Mission
      American universities, 52
      distortion of, 50

Modern universities, 20–25

"Monistic" university, 42

Multiversity
      minimal teaching-research link, 42
      modern, 27–28
      service role, 25

Mystical view of excellence, 15

N

National Aeronautics and Space Administration (NASA), 7

National identity, 23

National Institutes of Health (NIH)
      funding levels, 7
      industry collaboration, 52

National needs, 57–60, 73, 75, 78
National Science Foundation (NSF)
    funding levels, 7
    grant awards, 56
    research program comparisons, 74
    research purpose, 2
Natural sciences
    funding, 35, 50, 51
    research priority, 72
    teaching-research nexus, 40
Netherlands: research funding, 6
Newman, Cardinal, 23, 25, 26, 27, 28
NIH (see National Institutes for Health)
Nihilistic view of excellence, 15
NSF (see National Science Foundation)

O

Organisation for Economic Cooperation and Development (OECD), 6, 10
Organizational diversity, 78
Outcomes
    of research, 57
    view of excellence, 15
Oxford University, 15, 23

P

Peer review
    broadened, 77
    commercial interests, 7
    criteria for selection, 62
    in funding process, 55–56
    vs. national priorities, 58–60
Pentagon, 7
Philosophia, 36
Philosophical approach, 16–18, 28
Physical sciences
    funding distribution, 6, 7
    research concentration level, 11
    research differences, 33
Policy
    current directions, 8–11
    exclusivity, 35
    inclusivity, 11
    postwar, 2–3
    science vs. higher education, 5
    science vs. research, 50

W

West Germany: R&D funding, 5, 6
Wisconsin university model, 17
Wissenschaft, 36, 40
Wissenschaftsideologie, 21, 22, 37, 38
Word War II (see Postwar expansion)

ASHE-ERIC HIGHER EDUCATION REPORTS

Since 1983, the Association for the Study of Higher Education (ASHE) and the ERIC Clearinghouse on Higher Education, a sponsored project of the School of Education and Human Development at the George Washington University, have cosponsored the ASHE-ERIC Higher Education Report series. The 1988 series is the seventeenth overall, with the American Association for Higher Education having served as cosponsor before 1983.

Each monograph is the definitive analysis of a tough higher education problem, based on thorough research of pertinent literature and institutional experiences. After topics are identified by a national survey, noted practitioners and scholars write the reports, with experts reviewing each manuscript before publication.

Eight monographs (10 monographs before 1985) in the ASHE-ERIC Higher Education Report series are published each year, available individually or by subscription. Subscription to eight issues is $60 regular; $50 for members of AERA, AAHE, and AIR; $40 for members of ASHE (add $10.00 for postage outside the United States).

Prices for single copies, including 4th class postage and handling, are $15.00 regular and $11.25 for members of AERA, AAHE, AIR, and ASHE ($10.00 regular and $7.50 for members for 1985 to 1987 reports, $7.50 regular and $6.00 for members for 1983 and 1984 reports, $6.50 regular and $5.00 for members for reports published before 1983). If faster postage is desired for U.S. and Canadian orders, add $1.00 for each publication ordered; overseas, add $5.00. For VISA and MasterCard payments, include card number, expiration date, and signature. Orders under $25 must be prepaid. Bulk discounts are available on orders of 15 or more reports (not applicable to subscriptions). Order from the Publications Department, ASHE-ERIC Higher Education Reports, The George Washington University, One Dupont Circle, Suite 630, Washington, D.C. 20036-1183, or phone us at 202/296-2597. Write for a publications list of all the Higher Education Reports available.

1988 ASHE-ERIC Higher Education Reports

1. The Invisible Tapestry: Culture in American Colleges and Universities
   George D. Kuh and Elizabeth J. Whitt

2. Critical Thinking: Theory, Research, Practice, and Possibilities
   Joanne Gainen Kurfiss

3. Developing Academic Programs: The Climate for Innovation
   Daniel T. Seymour

4. Peer Teaching: To Teach Is to Learn Twice
   Neal A. Whitman

5. Higher Education and State Governments: Renewed Partnership, Cooperation, or Competition?
   Edward R. Hines

6. Entrepreneurship and Higher Education: Lessons for Colleges, Universities, and Industry
   James S. Fairweather

7. Planning for Microcomputers in Higher Education: Strategies for the Next Generation
   Reynolds Ferrante, John Hayman, Jr., Mary Susan Carlson, and Harry Phillips

8. The Challenge for Research in Higher Education: Harmonizing Excellence and Utility
   Alan W. Lindsay and Ruth T. Neumann

1987 ASHE-ERIC Higher Education Reports

1. Incentive Early Retirement Programs for Faculty: Innovative Responses to a Changing Environment
   Jay L. Chronister and Thomas R. Kepple, Jr.

2. Working Effectively with Trustees: Building Cooperative Campus Leadership
   Barbara E. Taylor

3. Formal Recognition of Employer-Sponsored Instruction: Conflict and Collegiality in Postsecondary Education
   Nancy S. Nash and Elizabeth M. Hawthorne

4. Learning Styles: Implications for Improving Educational Practices
   Charles S. Claxton and Patricia H. Murrell

5. Higher Education Leadership: Enhancing Skills through Professional Development Programs
   Sharon A. McDade

6. Higher Education and the Public Trust: Improving Stature in Colleges and Universities
   Richard L. Alfred and Julie Weissman

7. College Student Outcomes Assessment: A Talent Development Perspective
   Maryann Jacobi, Alexander Astin, and Frank Ayala, Jr.

8. Opportunity from Strength: Strategic Planning Clarified with Case Examples
   Robert G. Cope

1986 ASHE-ERIC Higher Education Reports

1. Post-tenure Faculty Evaluation: Threat or Opportunity?
   Christine M. Licata

2. Blue Ribbon Commissions and Higher Education: Changing Academe from the Outside
   Janet R. Johnson and Lawrence R. Marcus

3. Responsive Professional Education: Balancing Outcomes and Opportunities
   Joan S. Stark, Malcolm A. Lowther, and Bonnie M.K. Hagerty

4. Increasing Students' Learning: A Faculty Guide to Reducing Stress among Students
   Neal A. Whitman, David C. Spendlove, and Claire H. Clark

5. Student Financial Aid and Women: Equity Dilemma?
   Mary Moran

6. The Master's Degree: Tradition, Diversity, Innovation
   Judith S. Glazer

7. The College, the Constitution, and the Consumer Student: Implications for Policy and Practice
   Robert M. Hendrickson and Annette Gibbs

8. Selecting College and University Personnel: The Quest and the Questions
   Richard A. Kaplowitz

1985 ASHE-ERIC Higher Education Reports

1. Flexibility in Academic Staffing: Effective Policies and Practices
   Kenneth P. Mortimer, Marque Bagshaw, and Andrew T. Masland

2. Associations in Action: The Washington, D.C., Higher Education Community
   Harland G. Bloland

3. And on the Seventh Day: Faculty Consulting and Supplemental Income
   Carol M. Boyer and Darrell R. Lewis

4. Faculty Research Performance: Lessons from the Sciences and Social Sciences
   John W. Creswell

5. Academic Program Reviews: Institutional Approaches, Expectations, and Controversies
   Clifton F. Conrad and Richard F. Wilson

6. Students in Urban Settings: Achieving the Baccalaureate Degree
   Richard C. Richardson, Jr., and Louis W. Bender

7. Serving More Than Students: A Critical Need for College Student Personnel Services
   Peter H. Garland

8. Faculty Participation in Decision Making: Necessity or Luxury?
   Carol E. Floyd

1984 ASHE-ERIC Higher Education Reports

1. Adult Learning: State Policies and Institutional Practices
   K. Patricia Cross and Anne-Marie McCartan

2. Student Stress: Effects and Solutions
   Neal A. Whitman, David C. Spendlove, and Claire H. Clark

3. Part-time Faculty: Higher Education at a Crossroads
   Judith M. Gappa

4. Sex Discrimination Law in Higher Education: The Lessons of the Past Decade
   J. Ralph Lindgren, Patti T. Ota, Perry A. Zirkel, and Nan Van Gieson

5. Faculty Freedoms and Institutional Accountability: Interactions and Conflicts
   Steven G. Olswang and Barbara A. Lee

6. The High-Technology Connection: Academic/Industrial Cooperation for Economic Growth
   Lynn G. Johnson

7. Employee Educational Programs: Implications for Industry and Higher Education
   Suzanne W. Morse

The Challenge for Research in Higher Education   105

8. Academic Libraries: The Changing Knowledge Centers of Colleges and Universities
   Barbara B. Moran

9. Futures Research and the Strategic Planning Process: Implications for Higher Education
   James L. Morrison, William L. Renfro, and Wayne I. Boucher

10. Faculty Workload: Research, Theory, and Interpretation
    Harold E. Yuker

1983 ASHE-ERIC Higher Education Reports

1. The Path to Excellence: Quality Assurance in Higher Education
   Laurence R. Marcus, Anita O. Leone, and Edward D. Goldberg

2. Faculty Recruitment, Retention, and Fair Employment: Obligations and Opportunities
   John S. Waggaman

3. Meeting the Challenges: Developing Faculty Careers*
   Michael C.T. Brookes and Katherine L. German

4. Raising Academic Standards: A Guide to Learning Improvement
   Ruth Talbott Keimig

5. Serving Learners at a Distance: A Guide to Program Practices
   Charles E. Feasley

6. Competence, Admissions, and Articulation: Returning to the Basics in Higher Education
   Jean L. Preer

7. Public Service in Higher Education: Practices and Priorities
   Patricia H. Crosson

8. Academic Employment and Retrenchment: Judicial Review and Administrative Action
   Robert M. Hendrickson and Barbara A. Lee

9. Burnout: The New Academic Disease*
   Winifred Albizu Meléndez and Rafael M. de Guzmán

10. Academic Workplace: New Demands, Heightened Tensions
    Ann E. Austin and Zelda F. Gamson

*Out-of-print. Available through EDRS.